William Carew Hazlitt, John Suckling

The Poems, Plays And Other Remains

Vol. II

William Carew Hazlitt, John Suckling

The Poems, Plays And Other Remains
Vol. II

ISBN/EAN: 9783744709866

Printed in Europe, USA, Canada, Australia, Japan

Cover: Foto ©Thomas Meinert / pixelio.de

More available books at **www.hansebooks.com**

THE POEMS, PLAYS

AND OTHER REMAINS

OF

SIR JOHN SUCKLING

A NEW EDITION

With a Copious Account of the Author, Notes, and an
Appendix of Illustrative Pieces

VOL. II.

LONDON
FRANK & WILLIAM KERSLAKE, 13 BOOKSELLERS' ROW
1874

THE GOBLINS.

The Goblins. A Comedy. Presented at the Private-House in Black Fryers. By his Majesties Servants. Written by Sir John Suckling.

Printed in all the editions of Dodsley, except the last, from which it has been excluded on account of the appearance of the present new impression of Suckling's works. It is now given here with the notes of the commentators, and certain corrections, &c., by the present writer.

PROLOGUE.

WIT in a prologue poets justly may
    Style a new imposition on a play.
When Shakespeare, Beaumont, Fletcher, rul'd the stage,
There scarce were ten good palates in the age ;
More curious cooks than guests ; for men would eat
Most heartily of any kind of meat.
And then what strange variety ! each play
A feast for epicures, and that each day !
But mark, how oddly it is come about,
And how unluckily it now falls out ;
The palates are grown high'r,[1] number increas'd,
And there wants that which should make up the feast ;
And yet you're so unconscionable, you'd have
Forsooth of late, that which they never gave ;
Banquets before and after.——
Now pox on him that first good prologue writ,
He left a kind of rent-charge upon wit ;

---

[1] The later editions, viz., those of 1658 and 1696, read—

    "The palates are grown *higher*, number increas'd."—*Collier.*

[But *higher* is also the reading of edition 1648, and is undoubtedly the true one.]

Which if succeeding poets fail to pay,
They forfeit all their worth ; and that's their play :
You've ladies' humours, and you're grown to that,
You will not like the man, 'less boots and hat [1]
Be right ; no play, unless the prologue be
And ep'logue writ to curiosity.
Well, gentles, 'tis the grievance of the place,
And pray consider't, for here's just the case ;
The richness of the ground is gone and spent,
Men's brains grow barren, and you raise the rent.

---

[1] From the following passage in Fabian Philips's " Anti-
quity, Legality, Reason, Duty, and Necessity of Præ-emption,
and Pourveyance for the King," 4to, 1663, p. 384, we learn how
universally the fashion of wearing *boots* once prevailed in England : " Boots are not so frequently worn as they were in the
latter end of King James his Raign (when the Spanish embas-
sador, the Conde of Gondomar, could pleasantly relate, when
he went home into Spain, that all the citizens of London were
booted, and ready, as he thought, to go out of town) and that
for many years since all the men of the nation, as low as the
plowmen and meanest artizans, which walked in their boots, are
now with the fashion returned again, as formerly, to shooes and
stockings."

DRAMATIS PERSONÆ.

———o———

PRINCE, in love with Sabrina.
ORSABRIN, brother to the Prince, yet unknown.
SAMORAT, belov'd of Sabrina.
PHILATEL, }
TORCULAR, } brothers to Sabrina.
NASSURAT, }
PELLEGRIN, } Cavaliers, friends to Samorat.
TAMOREN, king of the thieves, disguis'd in devil's habit.
PERIDOR, ambitious of Reginella, disguised in devil's habit.
STRAMADOR, a courtier, servant to the Prince.
ARDELLAN, }
PIRAMONT, } formerly servants to Orsabrin's father.
PHONTREL, servant to Philatel.
SABRINA, belov'd by Samorat.
REGINELLA, in love with Orsabrin.
PHEMILIA, Sabrina's maid.

Captain and Soldiers.
Two Judges.
Two Lawyers.
Two Serjeants.
Gaoler.
Constable.
Tailor.
Two Drawers.
Fiddlers.
Clowns and Wenches.
Thieves, disguised in devils' habits, living underground by the
    woods.
Guard.   Attendants.

THE SCENE, FRANCELIA.

The Goblins.

———o———

ACT I. SCENE I.

Enter as to a duel, SAMORAT, PHILATEL, TORCULAR.

Samorat. BUT, my lords,
    May not this harsh business yet be
 left undone?
Must you hate me, because I love your sister?
And can you hate at no less rate than death?
 Philatel. No, at no less:
Thou art the blaster of our fortunes;
The envious cloud that darkens all our day.
While she thus prodigally and fondly throws away
Her love on thee, she has not wherewithal
To pay a debt unto the Prince.
 Samorat. Is this all?
 Torcular. Faith, what, if in short we do not think
 you
Worthy of her?
 Samorat. I swear that shall not make a quarrel.
I think so too; have urg'd it often to myself;
Against myself have sworn't as oft to her.
Pray, let this satisfy.

Philatel. Sure, Torcular, he thinks we come to talk.
Look you, sir. [*Draws.*]   And, brother, since his
          friend
Has fail'd him, do you retire.
    Torcular. Excuse me, Philatel,
I have an equal interest in this,
And fortune shall decide it.
    Philatel. It will not need; he's come.

Enter ORSABRIN.

Orsabrin. Mercury protect me! what are these?
The brothers of the highway!
    Philatel. A stranger, by his habit.
    Torcular. And by his looks a gentleman.
Sir, will you make one?   We want a fourth.
    Orsabrin. I shall be robb'd with a trick now!
    Samorat. My lords, excuse me; this is not civil:
In what concerns myself, none but myself
Must suffer.
    Orsabrin. A duel, by this light!——
Now has his modesty and t'other's forwardness
Warm'd me.   Gentlemen, I wear a sword,
                              [*Goes toward them.*
And commonly in readiness.   If you want one,
Speak, sir; I do not fear much suffering.
                              [*Speaks to Samorat.*
    Samorat. You're noble, sir;
I know not how t' invite you to it:
Yet there is justice on my side; and since
You please to be a witness to our actions,
'Tis fit you know our story.
    Orsabrin. No story, sir, I beseech you;
The cause is good enough as 'tis: it may
Be spoil'd i' th' telling.
    Philatel. Come, we trifle then.
    Samorat. It is impossible to preserve, I see,
My honour and respect to her:

And since you know this too, my lord,
It is not handsome in you thus to press me.
But come—— [*Torcular beckons to Orsabrin.*
  Orsabrin. O! I understand you, sir. [*Exeunt.*
                    [*Philatel and Samorat fight.*
  Philatel. In posture still!
              [*Samorat receives a slight wound.*
O, you're mortal then, it seems.
  Samorat. Thou hast undone thyself, rash man;
For with this blood thou hast let out a spirit
Will vex thee to thy grave.
    [*Fight again; Samorat takes away Philatel's sword,
      and takes breath, then gives it him.*
  Samorat. I am cool again. Here, my lord—
And let this present bind your friendship.
  Philatel. Yes, thus—— [*Runs at him.*
  Samorat. Treacherous and low!

Enter ORSABRIN.

  Orsabrin. I have drill'd my gentleman. I have made
As many holes in him as would sink
A ship royal in sight of the haven. How now?
            [*Samorat upon his knee.*
'Sfoot, yonder's another going that way too.
Now have I forgot of which side I'm on!
No matter: I'll help the weakest:
There's some justice in that.
  Philatel. The villain sure has slain my brother.
If I have any friends above, guide now
My hand unto his heart!
  [*Orsabrin puts it by; runs at him. Samorat steps in.*
  Samorat. Hold, noble youth;
Destroy me not with kindness! Men will say
He could have kill'd me, and that in justice
Should not be. For honour's sake,
Leave us together.

Orsabrin. 'Tis not my business, fighting : [*Puts up.*
Th' employment's yours, sir.   If you need me,
I am within your call.   [*Exit.*
   Samorat. The gods reward thee !
Now, Philatel, thy worst.
        [*They fight again, and close; Samorat forces his
            sword.*

Enter ORSABRIN.

Orsabrin. Hell and the furies are broke loose upon
   us !
Shift for yourself, sir.
        [*Fly into the woods several ways, pursued by
            thieves in devils' habits.*

Enter TORCULAR, *weak with bleeding.*

Torcular. It will not be : my body is a jade.
I feel it tire and languish under me.
Those thoughts came to my soul,
Like screech-owls [1] to a sick man's window.

Enter Thieves *back again.*   √

Thieves. Here, here !
        [*They bind him and carry him away.*
Torcular. O, I am fetch'd away alive !   [*Exeunt.*

Enter ORSABRIN.

Orsabrin. Now the good gods preserve my senses
   right,
For they were never in more danger !
I' th' name of doubt, what could this be ?

---

[1] So in "Othello"—

> "Oh, it came o'er me
> As doth the raven o'er th' infected house."—*Steevens.*

[Reed added a long quotation from Marston here, which, as
pointed out by Collier, was totally irrelevant.]

Sure, 'twas a conjuror I dealt withal;
And while I thought him busy at his prayers,
'Twas at his circle, levying this regiment.
Here they are again!

Enter SAMORAT.

Samorat. Friend—Stranger—Noble youth——
Orsabrin. Here, here!
Samorat. Shift, shift the place, the wood is dan-
gerous:
As you love safety, follow me.   [*Exeunt.*

Enter PHILATEL.

Philatel. They've left the place, and yet I cannot
find
The body anywhere.   Maybe, he did not
Kill him then, but he recover'd strength,
And reach'd the town.   It may be not too.
O that this hour could be call'd back again!
But 'tis too late;
And time must cure the wound that's given by fate.
                                        [*Exit.*

Enter SAMORAT, ORSABRIN.

Orsabrin. I' th' shape of lions too, sometimes,
And bears?
Samorat. Often, sir.
Orsabrin. Pray, unriddle.
Samorat. The wiser sort do think them thieves,
which but
Assume these forms to rob more powerfully.
Orsabrin. Why does not then the state
Set out some forces, and suppress them?
Samorat. It often has, sir, but without success.
Orsabrin. How so?
Samorat. During the time those levies are abroad,

Not one of them appears.   There have been,
That have attempted underground ; but of those,
As of the dead, there has been no return.
    Orsabrin. Strange !
    Samorat. The common people think them
A race of honest and familiar devils ;
For they do hurt to none, unless resisted.
They seldom take away, but with exchange ;
And to the poor they often give ;
Return the hurt and sick recover'd ;
Reward or punish, as they do find cause.
    Orsabrin. How, cause ?
    Samorat. Why, sir, they blind still those they take,
And make them tell the stories of their lives ;
Which known, they do accordingly.
    Orsabrin. You make me wonder, sir.
How long is't since they thus have troubled you ?
    Samorat. It was immediately upon
The great deciding day, fought 'twixt the two
Pretending families, the Tamorens and the Orsabrins.
    Orsabrin. Ha ! Orsabrins ?
    Samorat. But, sir, that story's sad and tedious :
We're ent'ring now the town, a place less safe
Than were the woods, since Torcular is slain.
    Orsabrin. How, sir ?
    Samorat. Yes.
He was the brother to the Prince's mistress ;
The lov'd one too.   If we do prize ourselves
At any rate, we must embark, and change
The clime : there is no safety here.
    Orsabrin. Hum !
    Samorat. The little stay we make,
Must be in some dark corner of the town ;
From whence (the day hurried to th' other world)
We'll sally out, to order for our journey.
That I am forc'd to this, it grieves me not ;
But, gentle youth, that you should for my sake——

Orsabrin. Sir, lose not a thought on that :
A storm at sea threw me on land, and now
A storm on land drives me to sea again.
   Samorat. Still noble !   [*Exeunt.*

Enter NASSURAT, PELLEGRIN.

Nassurat. Why, suppose 'tis a wench ;
You would not go with me, would you?
   Pellegrin. To choose—to choose !
   Nassurat. Then there's no remedy.
      [*Flings down his hat, unbuttons himself, draws.*
   Pellegrin. What dost mean ?
   Nassurat. Why, since I cannot leave you alive,
I will try to leave you dead.
   Pellegrin. I thank you kindly, sir, very kindly.
Now the Sedgly [1] curse upon thee,
And the great fiend ride through thee
Booted and spurr'd, with a scythe on his neck !
Pox on thee, I'll see thee hang'd first !
'Sfoot, you shall make none of your fine
Points of honour up at my charge :
Take your course, if you are so hot.
Be doing, be doing.   [*Exit.*
   Nassurat. I am got free of him at last :
There was no other way : h' has been
As troublesome as a woman that would be
Lov'd, whether a man would or not,
And has watch'd me, as if he had been
My creditors' serjeant ; if they should have dis-
    patch'd
In the mean time, there would be fine
Opinions of me. I must cut his throat
In earnest, if it should be so.   [*Exit.*

---

[1] [See Hazlitt's " Proverbs," 1869, p. 365.]

Enter PERIDOR, TAMOREN, *with other* Thieves,
    and TORCULAR.

                                    [*A horn sounds.*
Thieves. A prize ! A prize ! A prize !
Peridor. Some duel, sir, was fought this morning :
    this,
Weaken'd with loss of blood, we took ; the rest,
Escap'd.
Tamoren. He's fitter for our surgeon than for us ;
Hereafter we'll examine him.   [*Again a shout.*
Thieves. A prize ! A prize ! A prize !
            [*They set them down, Ardellan, Piramont.*
Tamoren.
        Bring them, bring them, bring them in,
        See, if they have mortal sin :
        Pinch them as you dance about,
        Pinch them, till the truth come out.
Peridor. What art ?
Ardellan. Extremely poor and miserable.
Peridor. 'Tis well, 'tis well, proceed ;
Nobody will take that away from me,
Fear not.   What country ?
Ardellan. Francelia.
Peridor. Thy name ?
Ardellan. Ardellan.
Peridor. And thine ?
Piramont. Piramont.
Peridor. Thy story?
Ardellan. What story ?
Peridor. Thy life, thy life.   [*Pinch him.*
Ardellan. Hold, hold : you shall have it. [*He sighs.*
It was upon the great defeat given by
The Tamorens unto the Orsabrins,
That the old prince, for safety of the young,
Committed him unto the trust of Garradan,

And some few servants more, 'mongst whom I fill'd
A place.
    Tamoren. Ha ! Garradan ?
    Ardellan. Yes !
    Tamoren. Speak out, and set me nearer.
So, void the place [*to Attend.*] Proceed.
    Ardellan. We put to sea, but had scarce lost the
      sight
Of land, ere we were made a prey to pirates :
There Garradan, resisting the first board,
Chang'd life with death, with him the servants too :
All but myself and Piramont.
Under these pirates ever since
Was Orsabrin brought up,
And into several countries did they carry him.
    Tamoren. Knew Orsabrin himself ?
    Ardellan. O, no, his spirit was too great : we durst
Not tell him anything, but waited for
Some accident might throw us on Francelia ;
'Bout which we hover'd often, and were near
It now ; but Heaven decreed it otherwise. [*He sighs.*
    Tamoren. Why dost thou sigh ?
    Ardellan. Why do I sigh indeed !
For tears cannot recall him : last night,
About the second watch, the winds broke loose,
And vex'd our ship so long, that it began
To reel and totter, and (like a drunken man)
Took in so fast his liquor, that it sunk
Down i' th' place.
    Tamoren. How did you 'scape ?
    Ardellan. I bound myself unto a mast, and did
Advise my master to do so ; for which
He struck me only, and said I did
Consult too much with fear.
    Tamoren. 'Tis a sad story.   Within there !
Let them have wine and fire.   But hark you.
                        [*Whispers.*

Enter Thieves, *with a* Poet.

Thieves. A prize! A prize! A prize!
Peridor. Set him down.
Poet. "*And for the blue,*   [*Sings.*
          Give him a cup of sack, 'twill mend his hue."
Peridor. Drunk, as I live! Pinch him, pinch him.[1]
   What art?
Poet. I am a poet,
A poor dabbler in rhyme.
Peridor. Come, confess, confess.
Poet. I do confess, I want money.
Peridor. By the description he's a poet indeed.
Well, proceed. Pinch him.
Poet. What do you mean?
Pox on you! Pr'ythee, let me alone.

           "*Some candles here!*
            And fill us t'other quart, and fill us,
            Rogue, drawer, t'other quart.
            Some small-beer.
            And for the blue,
            Give him a cup of sack, 'twill mend his hue."

Tamoren. Set him by, till he's sober.
Come, let's go see our duellist dress'd.   [*Exeunt.*

Enter Tailor, *two* Serjeants.

Tailor. He's something tall, and for his chin,
It has no bush below: marry, a little wool,
As much as an unripe peach doth wear;
Just enough to speak him drawing towards a man.
Serjeant. Is he of fury?

---

[1] "Pinch him, pinch him," is given in the old copies as a
stage direction; but the repetition and the sense (to say nothing
of the measure, which is very irregular) show that those words
are part of the text.—*Collier.*

Will he foin,[1] and give the mortal touch?

Tailor. O no, he seldom wears his sword.

Serjeant. *Topo* is the word, if he do;
Thy debt, my little myrmidon?

Tailor. A yard and half, I assure you, without
abatement.

Serjeant. 'Tis well, 'tis wondrous well:
Is he retir'd into this house of pleasure?

Tailor. One of these he's entered: 'tis but
A little waiting, you shall find me at
The next tavern.   [*Exit.*

Serjeant. Stand close; I hear one coming.

Enter ORSABRIN.

Orsabrin. This house is sure no seminary for
Lucreces.
Then the matron was so over-diligent:
And when I ask'd for meat or drink, she look'd
As if I had mistook myself, and call'd
For a wrong thing.   Well, 'tis but for a night;
. And part of it I'll spend in seeing of
This town, so famous in our tales at sea.

Serjeant. Look, look: muffled, and as melancholy
after't
As a gamester upon loss; upon him, upon him !

Orsabrin. How now, my friends; why do you use
me thus?

Serjeant. Quietly; 'twill be your best way.

Orsabrin. Best way, for what?

Serjeant. Why, 'tis your best way, because there
will be

---

[1] *i.e.,* Thrust in fencing. So in "The Merry Wives of
Windsor:" "To see the *foin.*" See note on this passage.—
Steevens.
Again in "The Return from Parnassus," act i. sc. 2—

"Then roister doister, in his oily terms,
Cuts, thrusts, and *foins,* at whomsoever he meets."

No other ; *Topo* is the word, and you
Must along.
 Orsabrin. Is that the word ?
Why, then, this is my sword.   [*Run away.*
 Serjeant. Murder, murder, murder ! h' has kill'd
The Prince's officer : murder, murder, murder !
 Orsabrin. I must not stay, I hear them swarm.
             [*Exit.*

Enter Constable, People.

 Constable. Where is he, where is he ?
 Serjeant. Here, here !
O, a man-mender, a man-mender !
H' has broach'd me in so many places,
All the liquor in my body will run out.
 Constable. In good sooth, neighbour,
H' has tapp'd you at the wrong end too ;
He has been busy with you here behind,
As one would say ; lend a hand, some of you,
And the rest follow me.   [*Exeunt.*

Enter ORSABRIN.

 Orsabrin. Still pursu'd ! which way now ?
I see no passage ; I must attempt this wall.
O, a lucky door, and open !   [*Exit.*
    Enters again.
Where am I now ?
A garden, and a handsome house !
If't be thy will, a porch to't, and I'm made ;
'Twill be the better lodging of the two.
        [*Goes to the porch.*

Enter PHEMILIA.

 Phemilia. O, welcome, welcome, sir. My lady
  hath
Been in such frights for you.

Orsabrin. Hum ! for me !

Phemilia. And thought you would not come to-
night ?

Orsabrin. Troth, I might very well have fail'd her.

[*Aside:*

Phemilia. She's in the gallery, alone in the dark.

Orsabrin. Good, very good.

Phemilia. And is so melancholy.

Orsabrin. Hum !

Phemilia. Have you shut the garden door?
Come, I'll bring you to her ; enter, enter.

Orsabrin. Yes, I will enter :
He who has lost himself, makes no great venter.

[*Exeunt.*

ACT II.

Enter SABRINA, ORSABRIN.

Sabrina. O, welcome !
Welcome, as open air to prisoners ;
I have had such fears for you.

Orsabrin. She's warm, and soft as lovers' language :
She spoke, too, prettily. Now have I
Forgotten all the danger I was in. [*Aside.*

Sabrina. What have you done to-day, my better part ?

Orsabrin. Kind little rogue ! I could
Say the finest things to her, methinks ;
But then she would discover me :
The best way will be to fall to quietly.

[*Aside. Kisses her.*

Sabrina. How now, my Samorat !
What saucy heat hath stol'n into thy blood,
And height'ned thee to this ? I fear you are
Not well.

Orsabrin. 'Sfoot ! 'tis a Platonic :
Now cannot I so much as talk that way neither.

[*Aside.*

Sabrina. Why are you silent, sir?
Come, I know you have been in the field to-day.
    Orsabrin. How does she know that?   [*Aside.*
    Sabrina. If you have kill'd my brother, speak:
It is no new thing that true love should be
Unfortunate.
    Orsabrin. 'Twas her brother I kill'd then! would I
      were
With my devils again.   I got well rid
Of them! that will be here impossible.

Enter PHEMILIA.

Phemilia. O madam, madam,
You're undone! the garden walls are scal'd,
A flood of people are entering the house.
    Orsabrin. Good! why here's variety of ruin yet.
                         [*Aside.*
    Sabrina. 'Tis so,
The feet of justice, like to those of time,
Move quick, and will destroy (I fear) as sure.
O sir, what will you do? there is no vent'ring forth.
My closet is the safest: enter there,
While I go down and meet their fury,
Hinder the search, if possible.   [*Exit.*
    Orsabrin. Her closet? yea, where's that?
And, if I could find it, what should I do there?
She will return.   I will venture out.   [*Exit.*

Enter the PRINCE, PHILATEL, PHONTREL,
Company, Music.

Philatel. The lightest airs; 'twill make them more
    secure.
Upon my life he'll visit her to-night.
                  [*Music plays, and sings.*
    Prince. Nor she nor any lesser light appears:
The calm and silence 'bout the place persuades me
She does sleep.

Philatel. It may not be : but hold,
It is enough, let us retire.
Behind this pillar, Phontrel, is thy place ;
As thou didst love thy master, show thy care :
You to the other gate ; there's thy ladder.　　[*Exeunt.*

Enter SABRINA.

Sabrina. Come forth, my Samorat, come forth,
Our fears were false, it was the Prince with music.
Samorat, Samorat !　He sleeps :—Samorat !
Or else he's gone to find me out i' th' gallery ;
Samorat, Samorat ! it must be so.　　　　[*Exit.*

Enter ORSABRIN.

Orsabrin. This house is full of thresholds and trap-
　　doors.
I have been in the cellar, where the maids lie too ;
I laid my hand, groping for my way,
Upon one of them, and she began to squeak.
Would I were at sea again i' th' storm !
O, a door : though the devil were the porter,
And kept the gate, I'd out.

Enter SAMORAT.

Orsabrin. Ha ! guarded ! taken in a trap ?
Nay, I will out, and there's no other but this——
　　　　　　　　[*Retires and draws, runs at him ;
　　　　　　　　　　another pass, they close.*
Samorat. Philatel in ambush, on my life !

Enter SABRINA *and* PHEMILIA *with a light.*

Sabrina. Where should he be ?　Ha !
Good heavens, what spectacle is this ? my Samorat !
Some apparition, sure !
　　　　　　[*They discover one another by the light, throw
　　　　　　　　away their weapons, and embrace.*

Samorat. My noble friend !
What angry and malicious planet govern'd
At this point of time?
    Sabrina. My wonder does grow higher.
    Orsabrin. That which governs ever:
I seldom knew it better.
    Samorat. It does amaze me, sir, to find you here :
How enter'd you this place ?
    Orsabrin. Forc'd by unruly men i' the street.
    Sabrina. Now the mistake is plain.
    Orsabrin. Are you not hurt?
    Samorat. No ; but you bleed.
    Orsabrin. I do indeed, but 'tis not here ; this is
A scratch : it is within, to see this beauty ;
For by all circumstance it was her brother
Whom my unlucky sword found out to-day.
    Sabrina. O my too cruel fancy !   [*Weeps.*
    Samorat. It was indeed
Thy sword, but not thy fault ; I am the cause
Of all these ills.   Why do you weep, Sabrina?
    Sabrina. Unkind unto thyself and me,
The tempest this sad news has rais'd within me
I would have laid with tears, but thou disturb'st me.
O Samorat, hadst thou consulted but with love
As much as honour, this had never been.
    Samorat. I have no love for thee, that hast not had
So strict an union with honour still,
That in all things they were concern'd alike ;
And if there could be a division made,
It would be found, honour had here
The leaner share : 'twas love that told me,
It was unfit that you should love a coward.
    Sabrina. These handsome words
Are now as if one bound up wounds with silk,
Or with fine knots, which do not help the cure,
Or make it heal the sooner. O Samorat,
This accident lies on our love like to

Some foul disease which, though it kill it not,
Yet will't destroy the beauty ; disfigure't so,
That 'twill look ugly to the world hereafter.
    Samorat. Must then the acts of fate be crimes of
      men ?
And shall a death he pull'd upon himself
Be laid on others ? Remember, sweet,
How often you have said it in the face
Of heaven, that 'twas no love, which length of time
Or cruelty of chance could lessen or remove.
O, kill me not that way, Sabrina,
This is the nobler. Take it, and give it
                    [*Kneels, and presents his sword.*
Entrance anywhere but here ; for you so fill
That place, that you must wound yourself.
    Orsabrin. Am I so slight a thing ? so bankrupt?
So unanswerable in this world that, being
Principal in the debt, another must
Be call'd upon, and I not once look'd after ?
Madam, why d'you throw away your tears
On one that's irrecoverable ?
    Sabrina. Why?
Therefore, sir, because he's irrecoverable.
    Orsabrin. But why on him? he did not make
      him so.
    Sabrina. I do confess my anger is unjust,
But not my sorrow, sir. Forgive these tears,
My Samorat ; the debts of nature must
Be paid, though from the stock of love.
Should they not, sir?
    Samorat. Yes :
But thus the precious minutes pass. and time,
Ere I have breath'd the sighs due to our parting,
Will be calling for me.
    Sabrina. Parting !
    Samorat. O yes, Sabrina! I must part, as day
Does from the world ; not to return, till night

Be gone, till this dark cloud be over.
Here to be found were foolishly to make
A present of my life unto mine enemy.
Retire into thy chamber, fair; there thou
Shalt know all.

    Sabrina. I know too much already.   [*Exeunt.*

Enter PHONTREL.

    Hold rope for me, and then hold rope for him.
Why, this is the wisdom of the law now: a prince loses
a subject, and does not think himself paid for the loss,
till he loses another.   Well! I will do my endeavour
to make him a saver; for this was Samorat.   [*Exit.*

Enter SAMORAT, ORSABRIN *bleeding.*

    Orsabrin. Let it bleed on. You shall not stir, I
    swear.

    Samorat. Now, by the friendship that I owe thee,
And the gods beside, I will. Noble youth,
Were there no danger in the wound, yet would
The loss of blood make thee unfit for travel.
My servants wait me for direction—
With them my surgeon; I'll bring him instantly.
Pray, go back.   [*Exeunt.*

Enter PHILATEL, Guard. *Places them at the door.*

    Philatel. There! You to the other gate;
The rest follow me.   [*Exeunt.*

Enter ORSABRIN, SABRINA.

    Sabrina. Hark! a noise, sir!
The tread's too loud to be my Samorat's.

Enter the Searchers *to them.*

    Searchers. Which way? which way?
    Sabrina. Some villany is in hand. Step in here,
sir: quick, quick.   [*Locks him in her closet.*

Enter PHILATEL, Guard, *and pass over the stage.*

Philatel. Look everywhere.
              [*Philatel dragging out his sister.*
Protect thy brother's murderer !
Tell me, where thou hast hid him !
Or, by my father's ashes, I will search
In every vein thou hast about thee for him.

Enter ORSABRIN.

Orsabrin. Ere such a villany should be,
    [*Orsabrin bounces thrice at the door; it flies open.*
The gods would lend unto a single arm
Such strength, it should have power to punish
An army of such as thou art.
  Philatel. O ! are you here, sir ?
  Orsabrin. Yes, I am here, sir.   [*Fight.*
  Philatel. Kill her.   [*She interposes.*
  Orsabrin. O ! save thyself, fair excellence,
And leave me to my fate.   Base !
           [*The Guard comes behind him,*
              catches hold of his arms.
  Philatel. So, bring him ! One !—the other is not far.
                 [*Exeunt.*

Enter SABRINA, PHEMILIA.

Sabrina. Run, run, Phemilia, to the garden walls,
And meet my Samorat. Tell him, O, tell him—
Anything. Charge him, by all our loves,
He instantly take horse, and put to sea.
There is more safety in a storm, than where
My brother is.   [*Exeunt.*

ACT III.

Enter PERIDOR *and the other* Thieves.

STRAMADOR *led in, they dance about him, and sing.*

Thieves. A prize !　A prize !　A prize !
Peridor. Bring him forth, bring him forth.

> *Welcome, welcome, mortal wight,*
> *To the mansion of the night.*
> *Good or bad, thy life discover ;*
> 　*Truly all thy deeds declare ;*
> *For about thee spirits hover,*
> 　*That can tell, tell what they are.*
> *Pinch him, if he speaks not true ;*
> *Pinch him, pinch him black and blue*

Peridor. What art thou ?
Stramador. I was a man.
Peridor. Of whence ?
Stramador. The court.
Peridor. Whither now bound ?
Stramador. To my own house.
Peridor. Thy name ?
Stramador. Stramador.
Peridor. O ! you fill a place about his grace,
And keep out men of parts, d'you not ?
Stramador. Yes.
Peridor. A foolish utensil of state
Which, like old plate upon a gaudy day,[1]

---

[1] " In the inns of court, there are four of these in the year ; that is, one in every term—viz., Ascension-day in Easter Term, Midsummer-day in Trinity Term, All Saints in Michaelmas Term, and Candlemas in Hilary Term. These were no days in court ; and on these days double commons are allowed, and musick formerly on All Saints and Candlemas-day, as the first

'S brought forth to make a show, and that is all :
For of no use you are.   Y'had best deny this.
 Stramador. O no!
 Peridor. Or that you do want wit,
And then talk loud, to make that pass for it.
You think there is no wisdom but in form,
Nor any knowledge like to that of whispers.
 Stramador. Right, right !
 Peridor. Then, you can hate,
And fawn upon a man at the same time :
And dare not urge the vices of another,
You are so foul yourself.   So the Prince
Seldom hears truth.
 Stramador. O, very seldom.
 Peridor. And did you never give his grace odd
   counsels ;
And when you saw they did not prosper,
Persuade him take them on himself?
 Stramador. Yes, yes, often.
 Peridor. Get baths of sulphur quick, and flaming oils ;
This crime is new, and will deserve it.
He has inverted all the rules of state ;
Confounded policy.   There is some reason why
A subject should suffer for the errors
Of his prince ; but why a prince should bear
The faults of 's ministers—none, none at all.
Caldrons of brimstone there !
 Thief. Great judge of this infernal place,
Allow him yet the mercy of the court.
 Stramador. Kind devil !

---

and last of Christmas.   The etymology of the word may be
taken from Judge Gawdy, who (as some affirm) was the first
institutor of those days ; or rather from *gaudium ;* because, to
say truth, they are days of *joy,* as bringing good cheer to the
hungry students.   In colleges, they are most commonly called
Gawdy ; in inns of court, *Grand Days ;* and in some places they
are called *Coller Days.*"—Blount's *Glossographia.*

Peridor. Let him be boil'd in scalding lead a while,
T'inure and prepare him for the other.
Stramador. O, hear me, hear me !
Peridor. Stay ! Now I have better thought upon't,
He shall to earth again ; for villany
Is catching, and will spread. He will enlarge
Our empire much; then we're sure of him
At any time. So, 'tis enough. Where's our governor?
[*Exeunt.*

Enter Gaoler, SAMORAT, NASSURAT, PELLEGRIN,
and three others in disguise.

Gaoler. His hair curls naturally: a handsome
  youth!
Samorat. The same. Is there no speaking with
  him ?   [*Drinks to him.*
He owes me a trifling sum.
Gaoler. Sure, sir, the debt is something desperate ;
There is no hopes he will be brought to clear
With the world ; he struck me but for
Persuading him to make even with heaven.
He is as surly as an old lion,
And as sullen as a bullfinch. He never
Ate, since he was taken, gentlemen !
Samorat. I must needs speak with him. Hark in
  thy ear.
Gaoler. Not for all the world !
Samorat. Nay, I do but motion such a thing.
Gaoler. Is this the business, gentlemen ?
Fare you well.   [*Run after him, draw their daggers,
                              and set one to his breast.*
Samorat. There is no choice of ways then. Stir
  not !
If thou but think'st a noise, or breath'st aloud,
Thou breath'st thy last. So, bind him now.
                              [*They bind the Gaoler.*
Undo quickly, quickly—his jerkin, his hat !

Nassurat. What will you do ? None of these beards
   will serve ;
There's not an eye of white in them.[1]
   Pellegrin. Pull out the silver'd ones in his,
And stick them in the other.
   Nassurat. Cut them, cut them out. The bush will
   suit
Well enough with a grace still.
   [*They put a false beard on the Gaoler, and gag him.*
Samorat. Desperate wounds must have desperate
   cures :
Extremes must thus be serv'd. You know your parts.
                    [*Exit in the Gaoler's habit.*
Nassurat. Fear not : let us alone.
                         [*They sing a catch.*
Some drink ! what, boy, some drink !

> *Fill it up, fill it up to the brink.*
> *When the pots cry clink,*
> *And the pockets chink,*
> *Then 'tis a merry world.*

> *To the best, to the best, have at her ;*
> *And a pox take the woman-hater.*
> *The Prince of Darkness[2] is a gentleman :*
> *Mahu, Mahu is his name.*

---

[1] *An eye* is a small shade of colour. So in " The Tempest,"
act ii. sc. I—
       " With *an eye* of green in't."—*Steevens.*

[2] This catch is probably not the production of Sir John Suckling,
but one much older than his time : in Shakespeare's " King Lear"
there is an evident allusion to it, act iii. sc. 4—
       " *The Prince of Darkness is a gentleman :*
         Modo he's call'd, and *Mahu.*"

Unless the present performance was written from the hints in
" King Lear."

How d'you, sir?   [*To the Gaoler gagg'd.*
You gape, as if you were sleepy.   Good faith,
He looks like an *O yes !*[1]
     Pellegrin. Or as if he had overstrain'd himself
At a deep note in a ballad.
     Nassurat. What think you of an oyster at a low
          ebb?
Some liquor for him !   You will not be
A pimp for life, you rogue, nor hold
A door to save a gentleman.   You are—
Pox on him, what is he, Pellegrin?
If you love me, let's stifle him, and say
'Twas a sudden judgment upon him for swearing.
The posture will confirm it.
     Pellegrin. We're in an excellent humour ;
Let's have another bottle, and give out
That Ann, my wife, is dead.
Shall I, gentlemen ?
     Nassurat. Rare rogue in buckram,[2] let me bite thee.[3]
Before me thou shalt go out wit, and upon
As good terms as some of those in the ballad [4] do.

---

[1] *i.e.*, Like the crier of a court, whose custom it is to preface
what he has to say with a summons to attention in the French
language, *Oyez*, vulgarly pronounced *O yes.*   So in "The Merry
Wives of Windsor," act v. sc. 4—

> " Crier hobgoblin, make the fairy *O yes.*"

A man, whose jaws are extended by a gag, is not ill compared
to one who drawls out this introduction to a proclamation, with
his mouth wide open.—*Steevens.*

[2] Here seems to be an allusion to Falstaff's *rogues in buckram.*
—*Steevens.*

[3] A common phrase of the times.   Mercutio, in " Romeo and
Juliet," act ii. sc. 3, says—

> " I *will bite* thee by the ear for that jest."

And Sir Epicure Mammon, in " The Alchymist," act ii. sc. 3—

> " Slave, *I could bite* thine ear."

[4] *i.e.*, In " The Sessions of the Poets."

Pellegrin. Shall I so? Why then *foutre for the Guise.*[1]
Saints shall agree; and ours shall be
The black-ey'd beauties of the time.
I'll tickle you for old ends of plays.   [*They sing.*

> *A round, a round, a round :*
> *A round, a round, a round.*

Somebody's at the door !   [*Knocking at the door.*
Pr'ythee, pr'ythee : sirrah, sirrah, try thy skill.
Nassurat. Who's there ?

Enter a Messenger.

Messenger. One Sturgelot a gaoler here ?
Nassurat. Such a one there was, my friend, but he's
       gone
Above an hour ago.   Now did this rogue
Whisper in his heart, that's a lie ; and for that
Very reason I'll cut his throat.
Pellegrin. No, pr'ythee now,—for thinking ?
Thou shalt not take the pains ; the law shall do't.
Nassurat. How, how ?
Pellegrin. Marry, we'll write it over, when we're gone,
He join'd in the plot, and put himself
Into this posture, merely to disguise
It to the world.
Nassurat. Excellent ! Here's to thee for that conceit.
We should have made rare statesmen,
We are so witty in our mischief !
Another song, and so let's go,
It will be time.   [*They sing.*

> *A health to the nut-brown lass,*
> *With the hazel eyes : let it pass.*

---

[1] A proverbial expression during the League.

She that hath good eyes,
Has good thighs.
Let it pass, let it pass.

As much to the lively gray,
'Tis as good i' th' night as day;
She that has good eyes,
Has good thighs.
Drink away, drink away.

I pledge, I pledge: what ho! some wine,
Here's to thine,
And to thine,
The colours are divine.

But O the black, the black,
Give me as much again, and let't be sack.
She that has good eyes,
Has good thighs,
And, it may be, a better knack.

                       [*They knock.*

          Enter a Drawer.

Nassurat. A reckoning, boy.   There.   Dost hear?
                   [*Pay him the reckoning.*
Here's a friend of ours has forgotten himself
A little (as they call it):
The wine has got into his head,
As the frost into a hand; he is benumb'd,
And has no use of himself for the present.
   Boy. Hum, sir——   [*Smiles.*
   Nassurat. Pr'ythee, lock the door; and when he
Comes to himself, tell him he shall find us
At the old place.   He knows where.
   Boy. I will, sir.   [*Exeunt.*

      Enter ORSABRIN, *in prison.*

  Orsabrin. To die! Ay, what's that?

For yet I never thought on't seriously.
It may be 'tis—hum—
It may be 'tis not too.

Enter SAMORAT *as the* Gaoler ; *he undoes his fetters.*
Ha !   [*As amaz'd.*
What happy intercession wrought this change ?
To whose kind prayers owe I this, my friend ?
  Samorat. Unto thy virtue, noble youth ;
The gods delight in that as well as prayers.
I am——
  Orsabrin. Nay, nay,
Be what thou wilt, I will not question it.
Undo, undo.
  Samorat. Thy friend Samorat.
  Orsabrin. Ha !
  Samorat. Lay by thy wonder, and put on these clothes :
In this disguise thou'lt pass to the prison gates ;
There you shall find one that is taught to know
You : he will conduct you to the corner
Of the wood, and there my horses wait us.
I'll throw this gaoler off in some odd place.
  Orsabrin. My better angel !   [*Exeunt.*

  Enter PERIDOR *with the other* Thieves.

  Peridor. It is e'en as hard a world for thieves
As honest men : nothing to be got,
No prize stirring.
  1st Thief. None, but one with horses,
Who seem'd to stay for some that were to come,
And that has made us wait thus long.
  Peridor. A lean day's work, but what remedy ?
Lawyers, that rob men with their own consent,
Have had the same.   Come, call in our perdues,[1]
We will away——   [*They whistle.*

---

[1] So in " King Lear," act iv. sc. 7—
                " To watch—poor *perdu*—
                With this thin helm ? "
See notes on this passage in the ed. of 1778.—*Steevens.*

Enter ORSABRIN, *as seeking the horses.*

Orsabrin. I hear them now ; yonder they are.
Peridor. Hallo ! Who are these ? any of ours ?
Thief. No, stand close ; they shall be presently.
Yield, yield !
Orsabrin. Again betray'd !
There is no end of my misfortune !
Mischief vexes me like a quotidian ;
It intermits a little, and returns,
Ere I have lost the memory of
My former fit——
Peridor. Sentences, sentences !
Away with him,—away with him !   [*Exeunt.*

Enter Gaoler *and* Drawers *over the stage.*

Gaoler. I am the gaoler : undone, undone !
Conspiracy ! a cheat ! my prisoner, my prisoner !
                                                  [*Exeunt.*

Enter SAMORAT.

Samorat. No men, nor horses ! Some strange mis-
    take !
Maybe, th' are sheltered in the wood.

Enter PERIDOR *and other* Thieves, *examining the*
    young Lord TORCULAR *that was hurt.*

Peridor. And if a lady did but step aside, to fetch
A mask or so, you follow'd after still,
As if she had gone proud ?   Ha ! is't not so ?
Torcular. Yes.
Peridor. And if you were us'd but civilly in a place,
You gave out doubtful words upon't,
To make men think you did enjoy.
Torcular. O yes, yes.
Peridor. Made love to every piece of cri'd-up
    beauty,
And swore the same things over to them.
Torcular. The very same——

Peridor. Abominable !
Had he but sworn new things yet, it had been
Tolerable.
                    [*One of them reads the sum of the confession.*
    Thief. Let me see, let me see.   Hum !
Court ladies eight, of which two great ones.
Country ladies twelve ; termers all.[1]
    Peridor. Is this right ?
    Torcular. Very right.
    Thief. Citizens' wives of several trades :
He cannot count them.   Chambermaids
And country wenches, about thirty ;
Of which the greater part the night before
They were married, or else upon the day.
    Peridor. A modest reckoning !   Is this all ?
    Torcular. No.
I will be just t'a scruple.
    Peridor. Well said, well said.
Out with it.
    Torcular. Put down two old ladies more.
    Peridor. I' th' name of wonder, how could he think
        of old
In such variety of young ?
    Torcular. Alas ! I could never be quiet for them.
    Peridor. Poor gentleman !
Well, what's to be done with him now ?   Shall he
Be thrown into the caldron with the cuckolds ?
    Thief. Or with the jealous ? that's the hotter place.
    Peridor. Thou mistakest ;
It is the same : they go together still :
Jealous and cuckolds differ no otherwise
Than sheriff and alderman.   A little time
Makes the one the other.   What think you

---

[1] *i.e.,* Ladies who only visit the city in *term-time—i.e.,* when
the courts of justice are open, and young lawyers are willing to
qualify their dry studies with female dalliance.—*Steevens.*

Of gelding him, and sending him to earth
Again amongst his women ?   'Twould be
Like throwing a dead fly into an ant's nest ;
There should be such tearing and pulling,
And getting up upon him, they would worry
The poor thing to death !

  1st Thief. Excellent !
Or leave a string, as they do sometimes
In young colts.   Desire and impotence
Would be a rare punishment.

  Peridor. Fie, fie, the common disease of age :
Every old man has it.

     Enter TAMOREN *and more* Thieves, *leading*
             ORSABRIN.

A prize ! a prize ! a prize !

          [*Horns blow, brass pots beat on.*

  Orsabrin. This must be hell, by the noise !

  Tamoren. Set him down, set him down : bring forth
The newest rack and flaming pinching-irons.
This is a stubborn piece of flesh ;
'Twould have broke loose.

  Orsabrin. So, this comes of wishing myself
With devils again !

  Peridor. What art ?

  Orsabrin. The slave of chance ; one of Fortune's
    fools :[1]
A thing she kept alive on earth to make her sport.

  Peridor. Thy name ?

---

[1] So Romeo exclaims—

      "O, I am Fortune's fool !"

It seems to mean one who is unlucky.

  This is a plain allusion to the *fool* in the ancient moralities.
See note on "Measure for Measure," ed. 1778, vol. ii. p. 72.—
Steevens. It is very doubtful whether the author ever dreamt of
such "a plain allusion."—*Collier.*

Orsabrin. Orsabrin.

Peridor. Ha! he that liv'd with pirates?
Was lately in a storm?

Orsabrin. The very same.

Tamoren. Such respect as you have paid to me—
                    [*Whispers with Peridor.*
Prepare to revels, all that can be thought on;
But let each man still keep his shape.   [*Exit.*
                [*They unbind him.   All bow to him.*

[*Music and a dance.*]

Orsabrin. Ha! another false smile of Fortune!——
[*They bring out several suits of clothes and a banquet.*
Is this the place the gowned clerks do fright
Men so on earth with? Would I had been here before!
Master devil, to whose use are these set out?

Peridor. To yours, sir.

Orsabrin. I'll make bold to change a little.   Could
        you not   [*Takes a hat, dresses himself.*
Afford a good plain sword to all this gallantry?

Peridor. We'll see, sir.

Orsabrin. A thousand times civiller than men,
And better natur'd!

Enter TAMOREN, REGINELLA.

Tamoren. All leave the room.

Peridor. I like not this.   [*Exeunt.*

Tamoren. Cupid, do thou the rest!
A blunter arrow, and but slackly drawn,
Would perfect what's begun:
When young and handsome meet,
The work's half done.   [*Exit.*

Orsabrin. She cannot be
Less than a goddess, and't must be Proserpine.
I'll speak to her, though Pluto's self stood by—
Thou beauteous queen of this dark world, that mak'st

A place so like a hell so like a heaven!
Instruct me in what form I must approach thee,
And how adore thee.

    Reginella. Tell me what thou art first; for such a
      creature
Mine eyes did never yet behold!

    Orsabrin. I am that which they name above a man.
I' th' wat'ry elements I much have liv'd; and there
They term me Orsabrin.   Have you a name too?

    Reginella. Why do you ask?

    Orsabrin. Because I'd call upon it in a storm,
And save a ship from perishing sometimes.

    Reginella. 'Tis Reginella.

    Orsabrin. Are you a woman too?
I never was in earnest until now.

    Reginella. I know not what I am;
For like myself I never yet saw any.

    Orsabrin. Nor ever shall.   O! how came you hither?
Sure you were betray'd.   Will you leave this place,
And live with such as I am?

    Reginella. Why may not you live here with me?

    Orsabrin. Yes; but I'd carry thee where there is
A glorious light; where all above is spread
A canopy, studded with twinkling gems,
Beauteous as lovers' eyes; and underneath
Carpets of flow'ry meads to tread on:
A thousand thousand pleasures, which this place can
      ne'er
Afford thee.

    Reginella. Indeed!

    Orsabrin. Yes, indeed.   I'll bring thee unto shady
      walks,
And groves fringed with silver purling streams,
Where thou shalt hear soft-feather'd quiristers
Sing sweetly to thee of their own accord.
I'll fill thy lap with early flowers;
And whilst thou bind'st them up mysterious ways,

I'll tell thee pretty tales, and sigh by thee ;
Thus press thy hand, and warm it thus with kisses.
   Reginella. Will you indeed?
        [*Tamoren and Peridor above, with others.*
   Tamoren. Fond girl! Her rashness
Sullies the glory of her beauty : 'twill make
The conquest cheap, and weaken my designs !
Go part them instantly, and blind him as before.
Be you his keeper, Peridor.
   Peridor. Yes, I will keep him.
   Orsabrin. Her eyes like lightning shoot into my
     heart,
They'll melt it into nothing, ere I can
Present it to her ! Sweet excellence !

Enter Thieves, *and blind him.*

Ha! why is this hateful curtain drawn before my
     eyes?
If I have sinn'd, give me some other punishment :
Let me but look on her still, and double it !
O, whither, whither do you hurry me? [*Carry him away.*
   Peridor. Madam, you must in.
   Reginella. Ah me ! what's this?
Must !——   [*Exit.*

Enter other Devils.

   1*st Thief.* We have had such sport ! Yonder's the
rarest poet without, 'has made all his confession in
blank verse ; not left a god nor a goddess in heaven,
but fetch'd them all down for witnesses. He has
made such a description of Styx and the Ferry, and
verily thinks he has pass'd them ! Inquires for the
bless'd shades, and asks much after certain British
blades ; one Shakespeare and Fletcher : and grew so
peremptory at last, he would be carried where they
were.
   2*d Thief.* And what did you with him?

1st Thief. Mounting him upon a coal-staff,[1] which (tossing him something high) he apprehended to be Pegasus. So we have left him to tell strange lies; which he'll turn into verse; and some wise people hereafter into religion. 　　　　　　[*Exeunt.*

ACT IV.

Enter SAMORAT, NASSURAT, PELLEGRIN.

Nassurat. Good faith, 'tis wondrous well. We have e'en done
Like eager disputers: and with much ado
Are got to be just where we were. This is
The corner of the wood.
　　Samorat. Ha! 'tis indeed!
　　Pellegrin. Had we no walking fire,
Nor saucer-eyed devil of these woods
That led us? Now am I as weary as
A married man after the first week: and have
No more desire to move forwards than
A post-horse that has pass'd his stage.
　　Nassurat. 'Sfoot, yonder's the night too,
Stealing away with her black gown about her:
Like a kind wench that had stay'd out the last
Minute with a man.
　　Pellegrin. What shall we do, gentlemen?
I apprehend falling into the gaoler's hands
Strangely. He'd use us worse than we did him.
　　Nassurat. And that was ill enough, of conscience.
What think you of turning beggars?
Many good gentlemen have done't. Or thieves?
　　Pellegrin. That's the same thing at court: begging
Is but a kind of robbing the exchequer.
　　Nassurat. Look, four fathom and a half O O S

---

[1] [See Nares, ed. 1859, *in v. Colestaff.*]

In contemplation of his mistress.
There's a feast! you and I are out now, Pellegrin.
'Tis a pretty trick, this enjoying in absence!
What a rare invention 'twould be,
If a man could find out a way to make it real!
   Pellegrin. Dost think there's nothing in't, as 'tis?
   Nassurat. Nothing, nothing.
   Pellegrin. Didst never hear of a dead Alexander
Rais'd to talk with a man?
Love is a learned conjuror, and with
The glass of fancy will do as strange things!
You thrust out a hand; your mistress
Thrusts out another. You shake that hand:
That shakes you again: you put out a lip:
She puts out hers. Talk to her; she shall
Answer you. Marry! when you come
To grasp all this, it is but air.   [*As out of his study.*[1]
   Samorat. It was unlucky.
Gentlemen, the day appears: this is no place
To stay in: let's to some neighbouring cottage,
Maybe, the searchers will neglect
The nearer places, and this will best
Advance unto our safety.

Enter Fiddlers.

   Nassurat. Who are there?
   1st Fiddler. Now, if the spirit of melancholy should
     possess 'em.
   2d Fiddler. Why, if it should, an honourable retreat.
   Nassurat. I have the rarest fancy in my head!
Whither are you bound, my friends, so early?
   Fiddler. To a wedding, sir.
   Nassurat. A wedding! I told you so. Whose?
   Fiddler. A country wench's here hard by,
One Erblin's daughter.

---

[1] [This marginal note is not in eds. 1646–48.]

Nassurat. Good : Erblin ! the very place !
To see how things will fall out !   Hold ;
Here 's money for you : hark you,
You must assist me in a small design.
　Fiddler. Anything.
　Samorat. What dost mean ?
　Nassurat. Let me alone—
I have a plot upon a wench.
　Fiddler. Your worship is merry.
　Nassurat. Yes, faith,
To see her only.   Look you, some of you
Shall go back to th' town and leave us your coats ;
My friend and I are excellent at a little instrument,
And then we'll sing catches rarely.
　Pellegrin. I understand thee not.
　Nassurat.[1] Thou hast no more forecast than a
　　squirrel,
And hast less wise consideration about thee.
Is there a way safer than this ? dost think
What we have done will not be spread beyond
This place, ere 'tis light ?[2] should we now enter
Any house thus near the town, and stay
All day, 'twould be suspicious : what pretence have we?
　Pellegrin. He speaks reason, Samorat.
　Samorat. I do not like it.
Should anything fall out, 'twould not look well ;
I'd not be found so much out of myself,
So far from home, as this disguise would make me,
Almost for certainty of safety.
　Nassurat. Certainty !   Why this will give it us.
Pray let me govern once.
　Samorat. Well, you suffer'd first with me, now
'Tis my turn.

---

　[1] What follows is given to Pellegrin in the copy of 1658. The alteration was made in the edition of 1696.—*Collier.*
　[2] Some of the old copies read "with every light."—*Collier.*

Pellegrin. Pr'ythee, name not suffering.

Nassurat. Come, come, your coats ; our beards will
    suit
Rarely to them : there's more money ;
Not a word of anything, as you tender——

Fiddler. O sir——

Nassurat. And see you carry't gravely too—
Now, afore me ! Pellegrin's rarely translated.
'Sfoot, they'll apprehend the head of the bass-viol
As soon as thee, thou art so like it !
Only, I must confess, that has a little the better face.

Pellegrin. Has it so?
Pox on thee, thou look'st like, I cannot tell what.

Nassurat. Why, so I would, fool ;
The end of my disguise is to have none
Know what I am. Look, look, a devil

Enter a Devil.

Airing himself ; I'll catch him like a mole,
Ere he can get underground.

Pellegrin. Nassurat, Nassurat !

Nassurat. Pox on that noise, he's earth'd.
Pr'ythee, let's watch him, and see whether
He'll heave again.

Pellegrin. Art mad ?

Nassurat. By this light,
Three or four of their skins, and we'd rob.
'Twould be the better way. Come, come, let's go.
                          [*Exeunt.*

Enter Captain *and* Soldiers.

Captain. Let the horse skirt about this place ;
We will make a search within.   [*Exeunt.*

Enter again.

Now disperse ;
In the hollow of the wood we will meet again.

Enter NASSURAT, PELLEGRIN, SAMORAT,
Fiddlers.

Soldiers. Who goes there? Speak!
O, they are fiddlers! Saw you no men nor horse
In the wood to-day, as you came along?
Nassurat. Speak, speak, rogue.
   [*Nassurat pulls one of the fiddlers by the skirt.*
Fiddler. None, sir.
Soldiers. Pass on.   [*Exeunt.*
Nassurat. Gentlemen, what say you to the invention
 now?
I'm a rogue, if I do not think
I was design'd for the helm of state:
I am so full of nimble stratagems,
That I should have order'd affairs, and
Carried it against the stream of a faction
With as much ease as a skipper
Would laver[1] against the wind.   [*Exeunt.*

Enter Captain *and* Soldiers, *meet again.*

Captain. What, no news of any?
Soldiers. No; not a man stirring.

Enter other Soldiers.

Soho! away, away!
Captain. What! any discovery?
Soldier. Yes, the horse has stay'd three fellows,
Fiddlers they call themselves;
There's something in't; they look suspiciously:

---

[1] To *laver* or *laveer* is a nautical term, and signifies the same
as to *tack*, or to *make boards* against the wind. Dryden uses it
in his "Astræa Redux"—

  " How easy 'tis, when destiny proves kind,
   With full-spread sails to run before the wind;
   But those that 'gainst stiff gales *laveering* go
   Must be at once resolv'd and skilful too."—*Collier.*

One of them has offer'd at confession once or twice,
Like a weak stomach at vomiting,
But 'twould not out.
    Captain A little cold iron thrust down his throat
Will fetch it up. I am excellent at discovery;
And can draw a secret out of a knave
With as much dexterity as a barber-surgeon
Would a hollow tooth.
Let's join forces with them.   *[Exeunt.*

      ORSABRIN *discovered in prison, bound.*

  Orsabrin. Sure 'tis eternal night with me! would
    this
Were all too; for I begin to think
The rest is true, which I have read in books,
And that there's more to follow.

        Enter REGINELLA.

  Reginella. Sure this is he——   *[She unbinds him.*
  Orsabrin. The pure and first-created light
Broke through the chaos thus!
Keep off, keep off, thou brighter excellence,
Thou fair divinity: if thou com'st near
(So tempting is the shape thou now assum'st),
I shall grow saucy in desire again;
And entertain bold hopes, which will but draw
More and fresh punishment upon me.
  Reginella. I see y' are angry, sir:
But if you kill me too, I meant no ill:
That which brought me hither,
Was a desire I have to be with you
Rather than those I live with. This is all,
Believe it.
  Orsabrin. With me? O thou kind innocence,
Witness all that can punish falsehood,
That I could live with thee,
Even in this dark and narrow prison,

And think all happiness confin'd within the walls.
O, hadst thou but as much of love as I !

    Reginella. Of love ! What's that ?

    Orsabrin. Why, 'tis a thing that's had, before 'tis
      known :

A gentle flame, that steals into a heart,
And makes it like one object so, that it scarce cares
For any other delights, when that is present ;
And is in pain, when 'tis gone ; thinks of that alone,
And quarrels with all other thoughts that would
Intrude, and so divert it.

    Reginella. If this be love, sure I have some of it.
It is no ill thing, is it, sir ?

    Orsabrin. O, most divine ;
The best of all the gods strangely abound in it,
And mortals could not live without it :
It is the soul of virtue and the life of life.

    Reginella. Sure, I should learn it, sir, if you would
      teach it.

    Orsabrin. Alas, thou taughtest it me ;
It came with looking thus—

                  [*They gaze upon one another.*

Enter PERIDOR.

    Peridor. I will no longer be conceal'd, but tell
Her what I am, before the smooth-fac'd youth
Hath taken all the room up in her heart.
Ha ! unbound ! And, sure, by her !
Hell and furies ! What, ho ! within there—

Enter other Thieves.

Practise escapes ?
Get me new irons to lead him unto death.

    Orsabrin. I am so used to this, it takes away
The sense of it ; I cannot think it strange.

    Reginella. Alas ! he never did intend to go.
Use him, for my sake, kindly ; I was not wont

To be deni'd.   Ah me ! they are
Hard-hearted all.   What shall I do ?
I'll to my governor, he'll not be thus cruel.   [*Exeunt.*

Enter SAMORAT, NASSURAT, PELLEGRIN.

  Nassurat. 'Tis a rare wench, she i' th' blue stock-
    ings :
What a complexion she had, when she was warm !
'Tis a hard question of these country wenches,
Which are simpler, their beauties or themselves.
There's as much difference betwixt
A town lady and one of these,
As there is betwixt a wild pheasant and a tame.
  Pellegrin. Right :
There goes such essencing, washing, perfuming,
And daubing to th' other, that they are
The least part of themselves.   Indeed,
There's so much sauce a man cannot taste the
    meat.
  Nassurat. Let me kiss thee for that.
By this light, I hate a woman drest up to her
    height,
Worse than I do sugar with muscadine :
It leaves no room for me to imagine
I could improve her, if she were mine.
It looks like a jade, with his tail tied up
With ribands, going to a fair to be sold.
  Pellegrin. No, no, thou hatest it out of another
    reason.
  Nassurat. Pr'ythee, what's that ?
  Pellegrin. Why, th' are so fine, th' are of no use that
    day.
  Nassurat. Sirrah, didst mark the lass i' th' green
    upon yellow,
How she bridled in her head,

And danc'd—a stroke in and a stroke out,
Like a young fillet, training to a pace ?[1]
   Pellegrin. And how she kiss'd !
As if she had been sealing and delivering herself
Up to the use of him that came last :
Parted with her sweetheart's lips still
As unwillingly and untowardly,
As soft wax from a dry seal.
   Nassurat. True ; and when she kisses a gentleman,
She makes a curtsey, as who should say,
The favour was on his side.
What dull fools are we, to besiege a face
Three months for that trifle ?
Sometimes it holds out longer ;
And then this is the sweeter flesh too !

Enter Fiddlers.

   Fiddler. You shall have horses ready at the time,
And good ones too (if there be truth in drink),
And for your letters they are there by this.
   Samorat. An excellent officer !

Enter Wedding.

   Clown. Tut, tut, tut !   [*Dance in, at that time.*

   Enter Soldiers *muffled up in their cloaks.*
That's a good one, i' faith ! not dance ?
Come, come, strike up.
   Samorat. Who are those that eye us so severely ?
Belong they to the wedding ?
   Fiddlers. I know 'em not.
       [*Offer their women to them to dance.*

---

[1] Hitherto it has stood—

" Like a young filly *straining to pace,*"

which is neither sense nor metre : the copy of 1658 gives the
true reading, which is restored.—*Collier.* [But all the old
copies have *fillet,* not *filly,* as printed by Mr Collier.]

Clown. Gentlemen, will't please you dance?

Soldier. No; keep your women; we'll take out
others here.

Samorat! if I mistake not?

Samorat. Ha! betray'd! [*A bustle.*

Clown. How now! what's the matter? abuse our
fiddlers!

2d Soldier. These are no fiddlers.

Fools, obey the Prince's officers,

Unless you desire to go to prison too.

Samorat. The thoughts of what must follow disquiets not

At all; but tamely thus to be surpris'd

In so unhandsome a disguise. [*They carry him away.*

Pellegrin. Is't even so? Why then

" Farewell the plumed troops[1] and the big wars,

Which made ambition virtue."

Nassurat. Ay, ay; let them go, let them go.

Pellegrin. Have you ever a stratagem, Nassurat?

'Twould be very seasonable. What think you now?

Are you design'd for the helm of state?

Can you laver against this tempest?

Nassurat. Pr'ythee, let me alone, I am thinking for
life.

Pellegrin. Yes, 'tis for life, indeed; would 'twere
not!

Clown. This is very strange; let's follow after,

And see if we can understand it. [*Exeunt.*

Enter PERIDOR, ORSABRIN.

Peridor. A mere phantasm, rais'd by art to try
thee.

Orsabrin. Good kind devil, try me once more:

Help me to the sight of this phantasm again.

Peridor. Thou art undone.

---

[1] See " Othello," act iii. sc. 2.

Wert thou not amorous in th' other world?
Didst not love women?

    Orsabrin. Who did hate them?

    Peridor. Why, there's it : thou thought'st there was
No danger in the sin, because 'twas common.
Above the half of that vast multitude,
Which fills this place, women sent hither ;
And they are highliest punish'd still,
That love the handsomest.

    Orsabrin. A very lying devil this, certainly !

    Peridor. All that had their women with you,
Suffer with us.

    Orsabrin. By your friendship's favour, though,
There's no justice in that : some of them
Suffered enough, in all conscience, by 'em there.

    Peridor. O, this is now your mirth ;
But when you shall be pinch'd into a jelly,
Or made into a cramp all over,
These will be sad truths.

    Orsabrin. He talks
Oddly now ; I do not like it.   Dost hear?
Pr'ythee, exchange some of thy good counsel
For deeds.   If thou be'st an honest devil
(As thou seem'st to be), put a sword into my hand,
And help me to the sight of this
Apparition again.

    Peridor. Well, something I'll do for thee,
Or rather for myself.   [*Exeunt.*

Enter two other Devils.

    1*st Devil.* Come, let's go relieve our poet.

    2*d Devil.* How! relieve him !
He's released, is he not?

    1*st Devil.* No, no :
Bersat bethought himself at the mouth of the cave,
And found he would be necessary to our masque to-
    night.

We have set him with his feet in a great tub of water,
In which he dabbles, and believes it to be Helicon.
There he's contriving i' th' honour of Mercury
Who, I have told him, comes this night of a message
From Jupiter to Pluto, and is feasted here by him.

Enter Poet *and* Thieves.

Devil. O, they have fetch'd him off!
Poet. —— Querer per solo Querer,[1]
Or he that made the " Fairy Queen." [2]
  1*st Thief.* No, none of these :
They are by themselves, in some other place ;
But here's he that writ " Tamerlane." [3]
  Poet. I beseech you, bring me to him ;
There's something in his scene

---

  [1] Sir Richard Fanshawe who, in 1670, published a paraphrase
of a dramatic romance written in Spanish by Don Antonio de
Mendoza (1628).
  [2] Spenser.
  [3] This was Christopher Marlowe, whose tragedy of "Tamerlane" was [twice] published in 1590. The following extract
from the scene betwixt the emperors will show that it was, as
the poet asserts, "a little high and cloudy :"—

> " Now cleare the triple region of the ayre,
> And let the majestie of Heaven behold
> Their scourge and terrour treade on emperours :
> Smile stars that raign'd at my nativitie,
> And dim the brightnes of their neighbour lampes.
> Disdaine to borrow light of Cinthia,
> For I, the chiefest lampe of all the earth ;
> First rising in the east with milde aspect,
> But fixed now in the meridian line,
> Will send up fire to your turning spheares,
> And cause the sun to borrow light of you.
> My sword strooke fire from his coate of steele,
> Even in Bythinia, when I tooke this Turke,
> As when a fiery exhalation,
> Wrapt in the bowels of a freesing cloud
> Fighting for passage make[s] the welkin crack,
> And casts a flash of lightning to the earth ;
> But, ere I march to wealthy Persia,
> Or leave Damascus and th' Egyptian fields,
> As was the fame of Clymeus brainsicke sonne,
> That almost brent the axletree of heaven :

Betwixt the emp'rors a little high and cloudy;
I would resolve myself.

  1st Thief. You shall, sir.
Let me see—the author of the " Bold Beauchamps,"
And " England's Joy."[1]

> So shall our swords, our lances, and our shot,
> Fill all the ayre with fiery meteors :
> Then, when the skie shall waxe as red as blood,
> It shall be said, I made it red my selfe,
> To make me thinke of naught but blood and warre."

—[Dyce's edit. of Marlowe, 1850, i. 77.]

[1] For an account of the singular composition called "England's Joy," see Collier's "Bibl. Cat.," ii. 466–68. Ben Jonson alludes to it in the "Masque of Augurs," 1621 : "—— were three of those gentlewomen that should have acted in that famous matter of ' England's Joy,' in six hundred and three ?" There is a proverb, "As bold as Beauchamp," which Fuller supposes to have taken its rise from Thomas Beauchamp, Earl of Warwick, the first of that name who, in the year 1346, with one squire and six archers, fought with an hundred armed men, at Hogges, in Normandy, and overthrew them, slaying sixty Normans, and giving the whole fleet means to land.—See [Hazlitt's Proverbs, 1869, pp. 58, 59, and] Dugdale's "History of Warwickshire," p. 316. Drayton, in his "Poly-olbion," song the eighteenth, says of the time of Edward III. :—

> " Warwick, of England then high constable that was
> As other of that race, here well I cannot pass :
> That brave and godlike brood of Beauchamps, which so long
> Them Earls of Warwick held ; so hardy, great, and strong.
> That after, of that name, it to an adage grew,
> If any man himself advent'rous hapt to show,
> Bold Beauchamp men him term'd, if none so bold as he.
> With those our Beauchamps, may our Bourchers reck'ned be."

The old play of the "Three Bold Beauchamps" is mentioned in the first act of Beaumont and Fletcher's "Knight of the Burning Pestle." In " A Cast over the Water to William Fennor," by John Taylor, fo. ed., p. 162, is the following proof of "England's Joy" being a dramatic performance :—

> " And poor old Vennor, that plaine dealing man,
> Who acted ' England's Joy' first at the Swan,
> Paid eight crowns for the writing of these things,
> Besides the covers and the silken strings."

Poet. The last was a well-writ piece, I assure you ;
A Briton,[1] I take it, and Shakespeare's very way.
I desire to see the man.

   1st Thief. Excuse me ; no seeing here.
The gods, in compliment to Homer,
Do make all poets poor above, and we,
All blind below. But you shall confess, sir. Follow.

                                        [Exeunt.

Enter PERIDOR, ORSABRIN.

   Orsabrin. Ha ! light and the fresh air again ! The
      place   *[Peridor unbinds him, and slips away.*
I know too ; the very same I fought the duel in.
The devil was in the right : this was
A mere apparition ; but 'twas a handsome one ;
It left impressions here, such as the fairest substance
I shall e'er behold will scarce deface.
Well, I must resolve : but what, or where ?
Ay, that's the question. The town's unsafe,
There's no returning thither ; and then the port—

                      [Some pass over hastily.
Ha ! what means the busy haste of these ?
Honest friend ! dost hear ? No. What's the matter,
    pray ?   *[Orsabrin calls to one.*

Enter Clown.

   Clown. Gentlemen, gentlemen !
   Orsabrin. That's good satisfaction, indeed.
Pr'ythee, good fellow, tell me,
What causes all this hurry ?

---

   [1] [In the old copy *a Brittain*, upon which the former editors
(except Collier) have raised an absurd hypothesis, that there
was an allusion here to Nicholas Breton, as to whom copious
particulars are to be found in Corser's "Collectanea" and
elsewhere, and a still more absurd note, full of errors and
irrelevancies.]

Enter another.

Clown. One Samorat is led to prison, sir,
And another gentleman about Lord Torcular.
   Orsabrin. Ha! Samorat! There is no mean nor
     end
Of Fortune's malice! O, 'tis insufferable!
I'm made a boy whipp'd on another's back!
Cruel! I'll not endure't, by heaven;
He shall die for me. I will not hold
A wretched life upon such wretched terms.

Enter TAMOREN, PERIDOR, *and others.*

   Tamoren. Fly, fly, abroad; search every place, and
Bring him back. Thou hast undone us all
With thy neglect; destroy'd the hopes we had
To be ourselves again. I shall run mad
With anger! Fly, begone! [*Exeunt all but Tamoren.*

Enter REGINELLA.

My Reginella, what brings you abroad?
   Reginella. Dear governor! I have a suit to you.
   Tamoren. To me, my pretty sweetness? what?
   Reginella. You will deny me, sir, I fear. Pray,
     let me
Have the stranger, that came last night, in keeping.
   Tamoren. Stranger! Alas! he's gone, made an
     escape.
   Reginella. I fear'd he would not stay, they us'd him
So unkindly. Indeed, I would have us'd
Him better, and then he had been here still.
                      [*She weeps.*
   Tamoren. Come, do not weep, my girl:
Forget him, pretty pensiveness; there will
Come others every day as good as he.
   Reginella. O, never!
I'll close my eyes to all, now he is gone.

Tamoren. How catching are the sparks of love !
   Still this
Mischance flows more and more unfortunate.
I was too curious :
Come, indeed you must forget him :
The gallant'st and the goodliest to the eye
Are not the best.   Such handsome and fine shapes
As those are ever false and foul within.
   Reginella. Why, governor, d'you then put
Your finest things still in your finest cabinets ?
   Tamoren. Pretty innocence ! No, I do not; you
   see
I place not you there.   Come, no more tears.
Let's in, and have a mate at chess ;
" Diversion cures a loss, or makes it less."   [*Exeunt.*

ACT V.

Enter TAMOREN, PERIDOR, *and other* Thieves.

   Peridor. Cross'd all the highways, search'd all the
   woods,
Beat up and down with as much pain and diligence,
As ever huntsman did for a lost deer.
   Tamoren. A race of cripples are ye all :
Issue of snails, he could not else have 'scap'd us.
Now, what news bring you?
   Thief. Sir, we have found him out :
The party is in prison.
   Tamoren. How ! in prison ?
   Thief. For certain, sir,
It seems young Samorat and he
Were those that fought the duel t'other day,
And left our Torcular so wounded there.
For his supposed death was Samorat taken ;
Which when this youth had found,

He did attempt to free him, scaling the wall
By night ; but, finding it impossible,
Next morning did present himself
Into the hands of justice, imagining
His death, that did the fact, an equal sacrifice.
　　Tamoren. Brave Orsabrin !
　　Thief. Not knowing that the greedy law asks more,
And doth proscribe the accessory as well
As principal.
　　Tamoren. Just so, i' th' nick ! i' th' very nick of time !
　　Peridor. He's troubled.
　　Tamoren. It will be excellent.
　　Be all in soldiers' habits straight.
Where's Torcular?
　　Thief. Forthcoming, sir.
　　Tamoren. How are his wounds? Will they endure
　　　the air?
Under your gabardines[1] wear pistols all.
　　Peridor. What does he mean?
　　Tamoren. Give me my other habit and my sword.
I' th' least suspected way haste after me.
　　Thief. All?
　　Tamoren. All but Peridor. I will abroad.
My broken hopes and suff'rings
Shall have now some cure.
Fortune, spite of herself, shall be my friend ;
And either shall redress, or give them end. 　*[Exeunt.*
　　Peridor. I've found it out :
He does intend to fetch this stranger back,
And give him Reginella :
Or else—no, no, it must be that ;

----

[1] "Gabardine" (from Fr. *gaban* or galleberdine), "a rough Irish mantle, or horseman's coat ; a long cassock."—*Blount's Glossographia.*
　　"Gaban, a cloake of felt, for raynie weather ; a gabardine."
—*Cotgrave.*

His anger and the search declare it—
The secret of the prison-house shall out,
I swear.   I'll set all first on fire :
For middle ways to such an end are dull.   [*Exit.*

Enter PRINCE, PHILATEL, *and* Servant.

Servant. Since she has refus'd to speak with you, sir,
She will not look on any ; languishes so fast,
Her servants fear she will not live
To know what does become of him.
    Philatel. Sir, 'tis high time you visit her.
    Prince. I cannot look upon her and deny her.
    Philatel. Nor need you, sir ;
All shall appear to her most gracious.
Tell her, the formal part o' th' law
Must pass : but when it comes t' execute,
Promise her that you intend to interpose.
    Prince. And shall then Samorat live ?
    Philatel. O [no, he'll die.]
Nothing less !   The sentence pass'd,
His death shall follow without noise :
'Tis but not owning of the fact,
Disgracing for a time, a secretary[1]
Or so—the thing's not new—
Put on forgiving looks, sir, we are there——

Sabrina's   Chamber.

A mourning silence.   Sister Sabrina !
    Sabrina. Hence, hence, thou cruel hunter after life !
Thou art a pain unto my eyes, as great
As my dear mother had when she did bring
Thee forth ; and sure that was extreme,
Since she produc'd a monster.

---

[1] Alluding to the Queen of Scots' case and Davison's disgrace,
in compliment to the Stuarts.

Philatel. Speak to her yourself;
She's so incens'd against me, she will not
Welcome happiness, because I bring it !
    Prince. Fair ornament of grief, why are you trou-
        bled ?
Can you believe there's anything within
My power which you shall mourn for ? if you have
Any fears, impart them ; any desires,
Give them a name, and I will give the rest.
You wrong the greatness of my love to doubt
The goodness of it.
    Sabrina. Alas ! I do not doubt your love, my lord ;
I fear it : it is that which does undo me.
For 'tis not Samorat that's prisoner now !
It is the Prince's rival.
O ! for your own sake, sir, be merciful
How poorly will this sound hereafter,
" The Prince did fear another's merit so ;
Found so much virtue in his rival, that
He was forc'd to murder it, make it away " ?
There can be no addition to you, sir, by his death ;
By his life there will : you get the point of honour.
Fortune does offer here,
What time perchance cannot regain :
A handsome opportunity to show
The bravery of your mind.
    Prince. This pretty rhetoric cannot persuade me,
        fair,
To let your Samorat live for my sake :
It is enough, he shall for yours.
    Sabrina. Though virtue still rewards itself, yet here
May it not stay for that ! but may the gods
Show'r on you suddenly such happiness,
That you may say, " My mercy brought me this."
    Prince. The gods no doubt will hear when you do
        pray
Right ways ; but here you take their names in vain,

Since you can give yourself that happiness
Which you do ask of them.
    Sabrina. Most gracious sir, do not——
    Prince. Hold,
I dare not hear thee speak, for fear thou now
Shouldst tell me, what I do tell myself;
That I would poorly bargain for thy favours.
Retire, and banish all thy fears.
I will be kind and just to thee, Sabrina,
Whatsoe'er thou prov'st to me.   [*Exit Sabrina.*
    Philatel. Rarely acted, sir!
    Prince. Ha!
    Philatel. Good faith, to the very life.
    Prince. Acted! No, 'twas not acted.
    Philatel. How, sir!
    Prince. I was in earnest.
I mean to conquer her this way:
The other's low and poor.
    Philatel. Ha!
    Prince. I told thee 'twould be so before.
    Philatel. Why, sir, you do not mean to save him?
    Prince. Yes, I do.
Samorat shall be releas'd immediately.
    Philatel. Sure, you forget I had a brother, sir;
And one that did deserve justice at least.
    Prince. He did; and he shall have it.
He that kill'd him shall die:
And 'tis high satisfaction that. Look not:
It must be so.   [*Exeunt.*

     Enter STRAMADOR *and* PERIDOR.

    Peridor. No devils, Stramador.
Believe your eyes, to which I cannot be
So lost, but you may call to mind one Peridor.
    Stramador. Ha! Peridor! Thou didst command
      that day,
In which the Tamorens fell.

Peridor. I did ; yet Tamoren lives.

Stramador. Ha !

Peridor. Not Tamoren the prince (he fell indeed) ;
But Tamoren his brother, who that day
Led on our horse.   Young Reginella too,
Which is the subject of the suit you have
Engag'd yourself by oath the Prince shall grant.

Stramador. O, 'tis impossible !
Instruct me how I should believe thee.

Peridor. Why thus :
Necessity upon that great defeat
Forc'd us to keep the woods, and hide ourselves
In holes, which since we much enlarg'd,
And fortifi'd them in the entrance so,
That 'twas a safe retreat upon pursuit :
Then swore we all allegiance to this Tamoren.
These habits, better to disguise ourselves, we took
At first ; but finding with what ease we robb'd,
We did continue 'em, and took an oath,
Till some new troubles in the state should happen,
Or fair occasion to make known ourselves,
Offer['d] itself, we would appear no other.
But come, let's not lose what we shall ne'er
Recover—this opportunity.   [*Exeunt.*

Enter Nassurat *and* Pellegrin, *in prison.*

Pellegrin. Nassurat, you have not thought of any
Stratagem yet ?

Nassurat. Yes, I have thought.

Pellegrin. What ?

Nassurat. That if you have
Any accounts with heaven, they may go on.
This villanous dying's like a strange tune,
'T has run so in my head,
No wholesome consideration would enter it.
Nothing angers me neither, but that
I pass my mistress's window to't.

Pellegrin. Troth, that's unkind.
I have something troubles me too.
    Nassurat. What's that?
    Pellegrin. The people will say, as we go along,
Thou art the properer fellow.   Then I break
An appointment with a merchant's wife :
But who can help it, Nassurat ?
    Nassurat. Yea, who can help it indeed !
She's to blame though, faith, if she does not
Bear with thee, considering the occasion.
    Pellegrin. Considering the occasion, as you say,
A man would think he might be borne with.
There's a scrivener I should have paid
Some money to, upon my word ; but——

    Enter ORSABRIN, SAMORAT, Prince's Servants, *with*
            Samorat's releasement.

    Orsabrin. By fair Sabrina's name, I conjure you
Not to refuse the mercy of the Prince.
    Samorat. It is resolv'd, sir.   You know my answer
    Orsabrin. Whither am I fallen !
I think, if I should live a little longer,
I should be made the cause of all the mischief
Which should arise to the world.
Hither I came to save a friend,
And by a sleight of fortune I destroy him.
My very ways to good prove ills.
Sure, I can look a man into misfortune !
The plague's so great within me, 'tis infectious.
O, I am weary of myself.
Sir, I beseech you, yet accept of it ;
For I shall be this way a sufferer
And an executioner too.
    Samorat. I beg of thee, no more ;
Thou dost beget in me desire to live :
For when I find how much I am behind
In noble acts of friendship, I cannot

Choose but wish for longer time, that I might
Struggle with thee for what thou hast too
Clearly now got from me, the point of honour.
O, it is wisdom and great thrift to die :
For who with such a debt of friendship and
Of love, as you and my Sabrina must
Expect from me, could e'er subsist ?
    Nassurat. They are complimenting ;
'Sfoot, they make no more of it,
Than if 'twere who should go in first at door.
I think, Pellegrin, as you and I
Have cast it up, it comes to something more !

Enter Messenger.

    Messenger. Gentlemen, prepare ; the court is sitting.
    Samorat. Friends, this is no time for ceremony ;
But what a rack have I within me to see
You suffer ! and yet I hope the Prince
Will let his anger die in me, not take
The forfeiture of you.
    Nassurat. If he should, Pellegrin and I are
Resolv'd, and are ready—all but our speeches
To the people ; and those will not trouble us
Much, for we intend not to trouble them.   [*Exeunt.*

Enter Prince, Philatel, and Attendants.

    Prince. Not accept it ! Lose this way too !—
What shall I do ? he makes advantages
Of mine ; and, like a skilful tennis-player,
Returns my very best with excellent design.
It must not be. Bring to the closet here above
The chief of the jury : I'll try another way. [*Exeunt.*

Enter Judges, Lawyers, Samorat, Orsabrin,
Nassurat, Pellegrin.

    Nassurat. Of all ways of destroying mankind, the
      judges
Have the easiest ; they sleep and do it.

Pellegrin. To my thinking now,
This is but a solemner kind of puppet-play :
How the devil came we to be actors in't ?
So, it begins.

    1*st Judge.* The Prince's counsel :
Are they ready ?

    Lawyer. Here.

    Judge. Begin then.   [*Prince and Philatel above.*

    Lawyer. My lords, that this so great and strange——

    Samorat. Most reverend judges, to save the expense
Of breath and time, and dull formalities of law,
I here pronounce myself guilty.

                  [*A curtain drawn ; Prince, Philatel,*
                        with others, appear above.

    Prince. Again he has prevented me !

    Samorat. So guilty, that no other can pretend a
      share.
This noble youth, a stranger to everything
But gallantry, ignorant in our laws and customs,
Has made perchance in strict severity
A forfeit of himself : but should you take it,
The gods, when he is gone, will sure revenge it.
If from the stalk you pull this bud of virtue,
Before't has spread and shown itself abroad,
You do an injury to all mankind ;
And public mischief cannot be private justice.
This man's as much above a common man,
As man's above a beast : and if the law
Destroys not man for killing of a beast,
It should not here for killing of a man.
O, what a mistake 'twould be !
For here you sit to weed the cankers out,
That would do hurt in the state : to punish vice ;
And under that you'd root out virtue too.

    Orsabrin. If I do blush, 'tis not (most gracious
      judges)
For anything which I have done ; 'tis for that

This much-mistaken youth hath here deliver'd.
'Tis true (and I confess) I ever had
A little stock of honour, which I still preserve :[1]
But that (by leaving me behind alive),
He now most cunningly does think to get from me ;
And I beseech your lordships to assist me,
For 'tis most fraudulent all he desires.
Your laws, I hope, are reasonable, else why
Should reasonable men be subject to them?
And then upon what grounds is he
Made guilty now? how can he be thought
Accessory to the killing of a man,
That did not know o' the fighting with him?
Witness all those powers which search men's hearts,
That I myself, until he beck'ned me,
Knew nothing of it. If for such a thing
A sacrifice must be, why man for man's enough ;
Though elder times, t'appease diviner justice,
Did offer up (whether through gallantry
Or ignorance) vast multitudes of beasts in sacrifice,
Yet numbers of us men we seldom hear of :
One single Curtius purg'd a whole state's sin.
You will not say the offence is now as great ;
Or that you ought to be more highly satisfied
Than heaven.
　　Prince. Brave youths !
　　Nassurat. Pellegrin, you and I will let our speeches
　　　alone.　　　　　　　　　　　　　　[*Aside.*
　　1st Judge. If that the law were of so fine a web,
As wit and fancy spin it out to here,
Then these defences would be just, and save you :
But that is more substantial, and
Of another make. And, gentlemen,
If this be all, sentence must pass.

---

[1] [Old copies, *preserv'd.*]

Enter Tamoren, Stramador.

Tamoren. Orsabrin !

Orsabrin. Ha ! who names me there ?

Tamoren. A friend.   Hear me.   I am an officer
In that dark world from whence thou cam'st,
Sent thus disguis'd by Reginella
Our fair queen, and to redeem thee.   [*Aside.*

Orsabrin. Reginella ! in the midst of all these ills,
How preciously that name does sound !

Tamoren. If thou wilt swear to follow me,
At the instant thou'rt releas'd,
I'll save thee and thy friends in spite of law.   [*Aside.*

Orsabrin. Doubt not of that.
Bring me where Reginella is, and if
I follow not, perpetual misery follow me !
It cannot be a hell where she appears.   [*Aside.*

Tamoren. Be confident.   [*Aside.*]   Behold, grave
  lords, the man   [*Goes out, and brings Torcular.*
Whose death questioned the life of these,
Found and recover'd by the thieves i' th' woods,
And rescued since by us, to rescue innocence.

Orsabrin. Rare devil !
With what dexterity he has raised this
Shape up to delude them.

Prince. Ha ! Torcular alive !

Philatel. Torcular !
I should as soon believe my brother
Were[1] in being too.

Torcular. You cannot wonder more to find me here,
Than I to find myself.

Nassurat. Come, unbind ; this matter's answer'd.

2d Judge. Hold ; they are not free : the law exacts
The same for breach of prison, that it did before.

---

[1] [Old copies, *near.*]

Orsabrin. There is no 'scaping out of Fortune's
    hands.
Dost hear! hast never a trick for this?
    Tamoren. Doubt me not; I have without at my
        command,
Those which never fail'd me; and it shall cost
Many a life yet, sir, ere yours be lost.

    Enter PRINCE, PHILATEL, *from above.*
STRAMADOR, PERIDOR, REGINELLA, *meet them below.*

    Prince. Stramador, you have been a stranger here
        of late.
    Stramador. Peruse this paper, sir; you'll find
There was good reason for't.
    Prince. How! old Tamoren's brother, captain
Of the thieves, that have infested thus
Our country!   Reginella too, the heir
Of that fear'd family! A happy and a strange discovery!
    Tamoren. Peridor and Reginella!   The villain
Has betray'd me.
    Reginella. 'Tis Orsabrin; they have kept their words.
    Orsabrin. Reginella! she is a woman then.
O, let me go!
    Gaoler. You do forget, sure, what you are.
    Orsabrin. I do indeed: O, to unriddle now!
    Stramador. And to this man you owe it, sir:
You find an engagement to him there;
And I must hope you'll make me just to him.
    Prince. He does deserve it; seize on him.
    Tamoren. Nay, then, all truths must out,
That I am lost, and forfeit to the law,
I do confess; yet since to save this prince——
    Prince. Prince!
    Orsabrin. Our Mephostophiles is mad.[1]

---

[1] This was the familiar spirit of Dr Faustus.   See a note on
"The Merry Wives of Windsor," act i. sc. I.—*Steevens.*

Tamoren. Yes, Prince, this is the Orsabrin.
Orsabrin. Ha!
Tamoren. So long ago supposed lost—your brother,
  sir.
Fetch in there Ardellan and Piramont.

Enter ARDELLAN *and* PIRAMONT.

Nassurat. What mad planet rules this day!
Ardellan and Piramont!
Orsabrin. The devil's wanton,
And abuses all mankind to-day.
  Tamoren. These faces are well known to all Fran-
    celians!
Now let them tell the rest.
  Piramont. My noble master living! found in Fran-
    celia!
  Ardellan. The gods have satisfied our tedious
    hopes.
  Philatel. Some imposture!
  Orsabrin. A new design of Fortune:
I dare not trust it.
  Tamoren. Why speak ye not?
  Piramont. I am so full of joy, it will not out.
Know, ye Francelians,
When Sanborn's fatal field was fought,
So desperate were the hopes of Orsabrin,
That 'twas thought fit to send away this prince,
And give him safety in another clime;
That, spite of an ill day, an Orsabrin might be
Preserv'd alive. This you all know.
To Garradin's chief charge he was committed;
Who, when our bark by pirates was surpris'd
(For so it was), was slain i' th' first encounter:
Since that we have been forc'd to wait
On Fortune's pleasure.
And, sir, that all this time we kept

You from the knowledge of yourself,
Your pardon.   It was our zeal that err'd,
Which did conclude it would be prejudicial.

 Ardellan. My lords, you look, as if you doubted still.
If Piramont and I be lost unto your memory,
Your hands, I hope, are not.   Here's our
Commission : there's the diamond elephant,
That, which our prince's sons are ever known by,
Which we, to keep him undiscovered,
Tore from his riband on that fatal day
When we were made prisoners.
And here are those that took us,
Who can witness all circumstances,
Both how and when, both time and place ;
With whom we ever since have liv'd by force :
For on no kingdom, friend unto Francelia,
Did fortune ever land us, since that hour,
Nor gave us means to let our country know
We[1] liv'd.

 Tamoren. These very truths, when they could have
  no ends   .
(For they believ'd him lost), I did receive,
From them before ; which gave me now
The boldness to appear here, where I'm lost by law.

 Shouts within. { *Long live Prince Orsabrin !*
        { *Long live Prince Orsabrin !*

 Nassurat. Pellegrin, let's second this ;
Right or wrong, 'tis best for us.

 Pellegrin. Observe, observe !

 Prince. What shouts are those ?

 Stramador. Soldiers of Tamoren's, the first ;
The second was the people's, who
Much press to see their long-lost prince.

 Philatel. Sir, 'tis most evident, and all agrees.
This was his colour'd hair,

---

     [1] [Old copies, *He.*]

His hair,[1] though altered much with time.
You wear too strange a face upon this news ;
Sir, you have found a brother :
I, Torcular : the kingdom, happiness.
For here the plague of robberies will end.
It is a glorious day.
 Prince. It is indeed ! I am amaz'd, not sad ;
Wonder does keep the passage so, nothing will out.
Brother (for so my kindred stars will have it),
I here receive you as the bounty of
The gods—a blessing I did not expect.
And in return to them this day Francelia
Ever shall keep holy.
 Orsabrin. Fortune, by much abusing me, has so
Dulled my faith, I cannot credit anything.
I know not how to own such happiness.
 Prince. Let not your doubts lessen your joys :
If you have had disasters heretofore,
They were but given to heighten what's to come.
 Nassurat. Here's as strange a turn, as if 'twere the
  fifth
Act in a play !
 Pellegrin. I'm sure 'tis a good turn for us.
 Orsabrin. Sir, why stands that lady so neglected there,
That does deserve to be the business[2] of mankind ?
O ye gods ! since you'll be kind
And bountiful, let it be here.
As fearfully as jealous husbands ask
After some secrets, which they dare not know,
Or as forbidden lovers meet i' th' night,
Come I to thee (and 'tis no ill sign this,
Since flames, when they burn highest, tremble most),
O, should she now deny me !

---

[1] [Old copies, *air*. But the allusion is still to the *hair*.]
[2] [This word, if the true one, should mean here the object of
universal attention.]

Reginella. I know not perfectly what all this means;
But I do find some happiness is near,
And I am pleas'd, because I see you are.
 Orsabrin. She understands me not !—
 Prince. He seems t' have passion for her.
 Tamoren. Sir, in my dark commands these flames broke out
Equally violent, at first sight ; and 'twas
The hope I had to reconcile myself.
 Orsabrin. It is a holy magic, that will make
Of you and I but one.
 Reginella. Anything that you
Would ask me, sure I might grant.
 Orsabrin. Hark, gentlemen, she does consent,
What wants there else ?
 Peridor. My hopes grow cold ; I have undone my-
  self.   [*Aside.*
 Prince. Nothing : we all join in this ; the long-liv'd feud
Between the families here dies. This day
The hymenæal torches shall burn bright,—
So bright, that they shall dim the light
Of all that went before. See, Sabrina too !

     Enter SABRINA.

 Tamoren. Sir, I must have much of pardon,
Not for myself alone, but for all mine.
 Prince. Rise ! hadst thou not deserv'd what now
  thou su'st for,
This day should know no clouds.
       [*Peridor kneels to Tamoren.*
 Tamoren. Taught by the Prince's mercy, I forgive too.
 Sabrina. Frighted hither, sir !   [*To Samorat.*
They told me you would not accept the Prince's mercy.

Samorat. Art thou not further yet in thy intelligence.
See, thy brother lives !
 Sabrina. My brother !
 Torcular. And 'tis the least of wonders has fall'n
  out.
 Orsabrin. Yes, such a one as you are, fair ;
            [*To Reginella.*
And you shall be acquainted.
 Samorat. O, could your hate, my lords, now,
       [*To Philatel and Torcular.*
Or your love die !   [*To Prince.*
 Philatel. Thy merit has prevail'd with me.
 Torcular. And me.
 Prince. And has almost with me.
Samorat, thou dost not doubt thy mistress' constancy ?
 Samorat. No, sir.
 Prince. Then I will beg of her,
That, till the sun returns to visit us,
She will not give away herself for ever.
Although my hopes are faint,
Yet I would have 'em hopes ;
And in such jolly hours as now attend us,
I would not be a desperate thing,
One made up wholly of despair.
 Sabrina. You, that so freely gave me Samorat's
  life,
Which was in danger,
Most justly may be suffer'd to attempt
Upon my love, which is in none.
 Prince. What says my noble rival ?
 Samorat. Sir, you are kind in this, and wisely do
Provide I should not surfeit : for here is happiness
Enough besides, to last the sun's return.
 Nassurat. You and I are but savers with all this,
  Pellegrin ;
But, by the Lord, 'tis well we came off as
We did : all was at stake.

Prince. Come, no more whispers here :
Let's in, and there unriddle to each other,
For I have much to ask.
    Orsabrin. A life ! a friend ! a brother ! a mistress !
    O, what a day was here ! Gently my joys distil,
    Lest you should break the vessel you should fill.[1]

---

[1] The measure throughout this play is very irregular, and it
has been so confusedly printed in the old copies, that many
speeches of mere prose have been capriciously cut into verses of
various lengths. It was utterly impossible to attempt to restore
it in all instances, or if it could be done, perhaps the attainment
of the object would hardly reward the trouble.—*Collier.*

EPILOGUE.

———o———

AND how, and how, in faith—a pretty plot;
    And smartly carried through too, was it not?
And the devils, how? well; and the fighting?
Well too; —— a fool, and't had been just old writing.
O, what a monster-wit must that man have,
That could please all ₗwhich now their twelvepence
      gave!
High characters (cries one), and he would see
Things that ne'er were, nor are, nor ne'er will be.[1]
Romances, cry easy souls; and then they swear
The play's well-writ, though scarce a good line's there.
The women—O, if Stephen should be kill'd,
Or miss the lady, how the plot is spill'd!
And into how many pieces a poor play
Is taken still before the second day!
Like a strange beauty newly come to court;
And to say truth, good faith, 'tis all the sport.
One will like all the ill things in a play,
Another some o' th' good, but the wrong way;
So that from one poor play there comes to rise
At several tables several comedies.
The ill is only here, that 't may fall out
In plays as faces;[2] and who goes about
To take asunder, oft destroys (we know)
What all together made a pretty show.

---

[1] " Whoever thinks a faultless piece to see,
    Thinks what ne'er was, nor is, nor e'er shall be."
—Pope's " Essay on Criticism," l. 252.

[2] Mr Reed allowed it to be reprinted " In plays as *farces;*"
the sense is very obvious according to the old reading.—*Collier.*

BRENNORALT.

Brennoralt. A Tragedy. Presented at the Private House in Black-Fryers. By His Majesties Servants. Written by Sir John Suckling.

This is the altered version of the "Discontented Colonel," as noticed in the Memoir. For the full title of the original play, see Hazlitt's "Handbook," p. 582.

"Brennoralt," in common with Suckling's other dramatic pieces, is printed in all the old copies, especially that of 1658, very carelessly, and in a style not greatly superior to that of a penny chapbook.

THE ACTORS.

———o———

SIGISMOND, King of Poland.

MIESTA,
MELIDOR, } councillors to the King.
A Lord,

BRENNORALT, a discontent.

DORAN, his friend.

VILLANOR,
GRAINEVERT, } cavaliers and officers under Brennoralt.
MARINEL,

STRATHEMAN.

FRESOLIN, brother to Francelia.

IPHIGENE, young Palatine of Florence.

PALATINE OF MENSECK, Governor, one of the chief rebels.

PALATINE OF TORK, a rebel.

ALMERIN, a gallant rebel.

MORAT, his lieutenant-colonel.

FRANCELIA, the Governor's daughter.

ORILLA, a waiting-woman to Francelia.

RAGUELIN, a servant in the Governor's house, but spy to Brennoralt.

Gaoler.

Guard.

Soldiers.

THE SCENE, POLAND.

Brennoralt.

—o—

ACTUS I. SCŒNA I.

Enter BRENNORALT *and* DORAN.

Bren. I SAY, the Court is but a narrow circuit,
Though something elevate above the com-
mon ;
A kind of ants' nest in the great wild field,
O'ercharg'd with multitudes of quick inhabitants
Who still are miserably busied to
Get in what the loose foot of prodigality
As fast does throw abroad.

    Dor. Good !
A most eternal place of low affronts,
And then as low submissions.

    Bren. Right.
High cowards in revenges 'mongst themselves,
And only valiant when they mischief others.

    Dor. Stars that would have no names, but for the ills
They threaten in conjunction.

    Bren. A race of shallow and unskilful pilots,
Which do misguide the ship even in the calm,

And in great storms serve but as weight to sink it.
More, pr'ythee more.   [*To the*] *alarum within.*
'Tis music to my melancholy.

Enter Soldier.

   Sol. My lord, a cloud of dust and men, the senti-
nels
From the east gate discover;
And as they guess, the storm bends this way.
   Bren. Let it be.
   Sol. My lord?
   Bren. Let it be.   I will not fight to-day;
Bid Stratheman draw to the trenches.   On, pr'ythee,
on.
   Dor. The King employs a company of formal
Beards-men, who have no other proof of their
Long life, but that they're old.
   Bren. Right, and if they are wise,
'Tis for themselves, not others,
As old men ever are.   [*Alarum.*

Enter 2 Soldier.

   2 *Sol.* Coronel, Coronel;
The enemy's at hand, kills all the sentries:
Young Almerin leads them on again.
   Bren. Let him lead them off again.
   2 *Sol.* Coronel?
   Bren. Be gone!   If th' art afraid, go hide thyself.
   2 *Sol.* What a devil ails he?   [*Exit.*
   Bren. This Almerin's the ague of the camp:
He shakes it once a day.
   Dor. He's the ill conscience rather; he never
Lets it rest.   Would I were at home again.
'Sfoot, we lie here i' th' trenches, as if 'twere
For a wind to carry us into th' other world.
Every hour we expect—I'll no more of it!

Bren. Pr'ythee!

Dor. Not I, by heaven!

Bren. What, man! the worst is but fair death.

Dor. And what will that amount to? a fair epitaph, /
A fine account! I'll home, I swear.

Enter STRATHEMAN.

Str. Arm, arm, my lord!
And show yourself, all's lost else.

Dor. Why so?

Str. The rebels, like an unruly flood,
Roll o'er the trenches, and throw down
All before them.

Bren. Ha!

Str. We cannot make a stand.

Bren. He would outrival me in honour too,
As well as love; but that he must not do.
Help me, Stratheman.   *[Puts on armour.*
The danger now grows worthy of our swords;
And, O Doran, I would to heaven there were
No other storms than the worst tempest here!
                     [Exeunt.

Enter MARINEL, *throwing down one he carries.*

Mar. There!
The sun's the neatest surgeon I know,
And th' honestest; if thou recoverest, why so:
If not, the cure's paid—they have maul'd us.

Enter GRAINEVERT, *with another upon his back.*

Gra. A curse light on this powder! It stays valour,
Ere it is half-way on its journey: what
A disadvantage fight we upon in this age!
He that did well heretofore had
The broad fair day to show it in: witnesses
Enough; we must believe one another
'Tis night, when we begin? Eternal smoke

And sulphur smalky.   By this hand, I can bear
With thee no longer.   How now? dead, as I live !
                                 [*Finds that he is dead.*
Stol'n away just as he us'd to wench.
Well, go thy ways; for a quiet drinker
And dier, I shall never know thy fellow.   [*Searches*
These trifles too about thee?   *his pockets.*
There never was an honester poor wretch
Born, I think ; look i' th' t'other pocket, too.
Hum ! Marinel ?
   Mar. Who's that ?
   Gra. 'Tis I ; how go the matters ?
   Mar. Scurvily enough ;
Yet since our Colonel came, they've got no ground
Of us ; a weak sculler against wind and tide
Would have done as much.   Hark !
This way the torrent bears.   [*Exeunt.*

Enter FRESOLIN, ALMERIN, *and* Rebels.

   Fre. The villains all have left us.
   Alm.   Would they had left
Their fears behind them ! but come, since we must.

Enter BRENNORALT, *with* Soldiers.

   Bren. Ho ! Stratheman,
Skirt on the left hand with the horse,
And get betwixt these and that body ;
They're new rallied up for rescue.
                  [*Brennoralt charges through.*
   Dor.   They're ours !
I do not see my game yet.   [*Exeunt.*

   A shout within.   Enter BRENNORALT, DORAN,
             STRATHEMAN, MARINEL.

   Bren. What shout is that?
   Str. They have taken Almerin, my lord.
   Bren. Almerin? the devil thank 'em for't !

When I had hunted hard all day,
And now at length unherded the proud deer,
The curs have snatch'd him up.   Sound a retreat ;
There's nothing now behind.   Who saw Doran?
   Str. Shall we bring Almerin in ?
   Bren. No ; gazing's a low[1] triumph :
Convey him fairly to the king,
He fought it fairly.

Enter DORAN.

   Dor. What youth was that whom you bestrid, my
     lord,
And sav'd from all our swords to-day?   Was he
Not of the enemy?
   Bren.   It may be so.
   Str. The governor's son, Fresolin, his mistress'
     brother.   [*In Doran's ear.*
   Bren. No matter who.   'Tis pity the rough hand
Of war should early courages destroy,
Before they bud, and show themselves i' th' heat
Of action.
   Mar. I threw (my lord) a youth upon a bank,
Which seeking after the retreat I found
Dead, and a woman,—the pretty daughter
Of the forester, Lucilia.
   Bren. See, see, Doran, a sad experiment !
Woman's the cowardli'st and coldest thing
The world brings forth : yet love, as fire works water,
Makes it boil o'er, and do things contrary
To 'ts proper nature.   I should shed a tear,
Could I tell how !   Ah, poor Lucilia !
Thou didst for me what did as ill become thee.
Pray, see her gently buried.
Boy, send the surgeon to the tent—I bleed.
What lousy cottages they've given our souls !

---

   [1] [Old copies, *is low.*]

Each petty storm shakes them into disorder ;
And't costs more pains to patch them up again,
Than they are worth by much.   I am weary of
The tenement.   [*Exeunt.*

    Enter VILLANOR, GRAINEVERT, MARINEL, *and*
               STRATHEMAN.

    Gra. Villanor! welcome, welcome, whence camest
      thou ?
    Vil. Look, I wear the king's highway still on my
      boots.
    Gra. A pretty riding phrase, and how, and how ?
[Be] ladies cheap ?
    Vil. Faith, reasonable ;
Those toys were never dear, thou know'st ;
A little time and industry they'll cost ;
But, in good faith, not much : some few there are
That set themselves at mighty rates.
    Gra. Which we o' th' wise pass by, as things
O'er-valued in the market.   Is't not so ?
    Vil. Y' have said, sir.   Hark you, your friend and
      rival's married ! [1]
Has obtain'd the long-lov'd lady, and is such
An ass after't.
    Gra. Hum !   It is ever so.
The motions of married people are as of
Other naturals, violent : [2] gentlemen to the place,
And calm in it.
    Mar. We know this too, and yet we must be fooling.
    Gra. Faith, women are the baggage of life : they are
Troublesome, and hinder us in the great march,
And yet we cannot be without 'em.

---

    [1] [Old copies, *the rivals.*]
    [2] [Old copies read—
        " Other naturals : violent gentlemen to the place,
          And calm in it,"
in which there is an evident corruption ; nor is it clear where
it lies.]

Mar. You speak very well and soldier-like.

Gra. What? thou art a wit too, I warrant, in
Our absence?

Vil. Hum!   No, no, a poor pretender,
A candidate or so,—'gainst the next Sessions,
Wit enough to laugh at you here.

Gra. Like enough ; valour's a crime
The wise have still reproached unto the valiant,
And the fools too.

Vil. Raillery apart, Grainevert ;
What accommodation shall we find here?

Gra. Clean straw (sweetheart) and meat—
When thou canst get it.

Vil.   Hum! straw?

Gra.   Yes.
That's all will be betwixt incest ;
You and your mother Earth must lie together.

Vil. Pr'ythee, let us be serious ; will this last?
How goes affairs?

Gra.   Well.

Vil.   But well?

Gra. Faith, 'tis now upon the turning of the balance :
A most equal business betwixt rebellion
And loyalty.

Vil. What dost mean?

Gra. Why ! which shall be the virtue, and which
   the vice.

Vil. How the devil can that be ?

Gra. O, success is a rare paint, hides all the
   ugliness.

Vil. Pr'ythee, what is the quarrel?

Gra. Nay, for that excuse us ;
Ask the children of peace,
They have the leisure to study it,
We know nothing of it ; liberty, they say.

Vil. 'Sfoot, let the king make an act,
That any man may be unmarried again ;

There's liberty for them !   A race
Of half-witted fellows quarrel about freedom,
And all that while allow the bonds of matrimony !
   Gra. You speak very well, sir.

Enter KING, Lords, BRENNORALT.

   Mar. Soft ; the king and council.
   Gra. Look, they follow after like tired spaniels
Quest sometimes for company; that is, *concur ;* [1]
And that's their business.
   Mar. They are as weary of this sport
As a young unthrift of's land: any
Bargain to be rid on't.
Can you blame them ?   Who's that ?
   Mar. Brennoralt, our brave Colonel :
A discontent, but what of that ? who is not ?
   Vil. His face speaks him one.
   Gra.   Thou art i' th' right.
He looks still as if he were saying to
Fortune: Housewife, go about your business.
Come, let's retire to Barathen's tent.
Taste a bottle, and speak bold truths ;
That's our way now.
              [*Exeunt.   Manent King and Lords.*
   Mi. Think not of pardon, sir ;
Rigour and mercy us'd in states uncertainly,
And in ill times, look not like the effects
Of virtue, but necessity.   Nor will
They thank your goodness, but your fears.
   Mel. My lords ;
Revenge in princes should be still imperfect :
It is then handsom'st, when the king comes to
Reduce, not ruin.
   Bren. Who puts but on the face of punishing,
And only gently cuts, but prunes rebellion :

---

[1] [A *jeu de mot* seems to be intended.]

He makes that flourish which he would destroy.
Who would not be a rebel, when the hopes
Are vast, the fears but small?
    Mel. Why, I would not.
Nor you, my lord, nor you, nor any here.
Fear keeps low spirits only in ; the brave
Do get above it when they do resolve.
Such punishments, in infancy of war,
Make men more desperate, not the more yielding.
The common people are a kind of flies :
They're caught with honey, not with wormwood, sir.
Severity exasp'rates the stirr'd humour ;
And state-distempers turns into diseases.
    Bren. The gods forbid great Poland's state should be
Such as it dares not take right physic.   Quarter
To rebels?   Sir, when you give that to them,
Give that to me which they deserve.   I would
Not live to see it.
    3 *Lord.* Turn o'er your own and others' chronicles,
And you shall find, great sir,
" That nothing makes a civil war long-liv'd,
But ransom and returning back the brands,
Which unextinct kindled still fiercer fires."
    Mi. Mercy, bestow'd on those that do dispute
With swords, does lose the angel's face it has,
And is not mercy, sir, but policy
With a weak vizard on.
    King. Y' have met my thoughts,
My lords ; nor will it need larger debate.
To-morrow, in the sight of the besieg'd,
The rebel dies.   Miesta, 'tis your care.
The mercy of heav'n may be offended so,
That it cannot forgive : mortals' much more,
Which is not infinite, my lords.   *[Exeunt.*

    Enter IPHIGENE, ALMERIN (*as in prison*).
    Iph. O Almerin ! would we had never known

The ruffle of the world ! but were again
By Stolden banks in happy solitude ;
When thou and I, shepherd and shepherdess
So oft by turns, as often still have wish'd,
That we as eas'ly could have chang'd our sex,
As clothes.   But, alas ! all those innocent joys,
Like glorious mornings, are retir'd into
Dark sullen clouds, before we knew to value
What we had.

 Alm. Fame and victory are light
Housewives, that throw themselves into the arms,
Not of the valiant, but the fortunate.
To be ta'en thus !   [*To himself.*

 Iph. Almerin !

 Alm. Nipp'd i' th' bud
Of honour !

 Iph. My lord !

 Alm. Foiled ! and by the man,
That does pretend unto Francelia !

 Iph. What is't you do, my Almerin? sit still,
And quarrel with the winds, because there is
A shipwreck tow'rds, and never think of saving
The barque ?

 Alm. The barque ?   What should we do with
  that
When the rich freight is lost, my name in arms?

 Iph. Who knows what prizes are behind, if you
Attend and wait a second voyage?

 Alm. Never, never !
There are no second voyages in this ;
The wounds of honour do admit no cure.

 Iph. Those slight ones which misfortune gives
  must needs,
Else why should mortals value it at all?
For who would toil to treasure up a wealth,
Which weak inconstancy did keep, or might
Dispose of?

Enter MELIDOR.

Iph. O my lord, what news?

Mel. As ill as your own fears could give you;
The council has decreed him sudden death,
And all the ways to mercy are blocked up.

                              [*She weeps and sighs.*

Alm. My Iphigene!
This was a misbecoming piece of love:
Women would manage a disaster better.

                    [*Iphigene weeps and sighs again.*

Again? thou art unkind!
Thy goodness is so great it makes thee faulty:
For while thou think'st to take the trouble from me,
Thou giv'st me more by giving me thine too.

Iph. Alas! I am indeed an useless trifle;
A dull—dull thing: for could I now do anything
But grieve and pity, I might help. My thoughts   ʌ
Labour to find a way; but, like to birds
In cages, though they never rest, they are
But where they did set out at first.

Enter Gaoler.

Gao. My lords, your pardon. The prisoner must
    retire.
I have receiv'd an order from the king
Denies access to any.

Iph.   He cannot be
So great a tyrant.

Alm. I thank him; nor can he
Use me ill enough. I only grieve
That I must die in debt—a bankrupt! Such
Thy love hath made me: my dear Iphigene,
Farewell: it is no time for ceremony.
Show me the way I must.   [*Exit.*

Iph. Grief strove with such disorder to get out,
It stopp'd the passage, and sent back my words
That were already on the place.

Mel. Stay, there is yet a way.

Iph. O, speak it !

Mel. But there is
Danger in't, Iphigene—to thee high danger.

Iph. Fright children in the dark with that, and let
Me know it. There is no such thing in nature,
If Almerin be lost.

Mel. Thus then ; you must
Be taken pris'ner too, and by exchange
Save Almerin.   [*Aside.*

Iph.   How can that be ?   [*Aside.*

Mel. Why—   [*Studies.*
Step in, and pray him set his hand about
                                          [*To the Gaoler.*
This distance ; his seal too——

Gao. My lord, I know not what this is.

Mel. Settling of money-business, fool, betwixt us.

Gao. If 't be no more——   [*Exit.*

Mel. Tell him that Iphigene and I desire it :
I'll send by Strathocles his servant
A letter to Morat thus sign'd and seal'd,
That shall inform the sudden execution ;
Command him, as the only means to save
His life, to sally out this night upon
The quarters, and endeavour prisoners.
Name you as most secure and slightest guarded,
Best pledge of safety ; but charge him
That he kill not any, if it be avoidable ;
Lest 't should enrage the king yet more,
And make his death more certain.

Enter Gaoler *with the writing.*

Gao. He understands you not, he says, but he
Has sent it.

Mel. So.

Iph. But should Morat mistrust now ?
Or this miscarry ?

Mel. Come :
Leave it to me ; I'll take the pilot's part ;
And reach the port, or perish in the art.   [*Exeunt.*

ACTUS II. SCŒNA I.

Enter ALMERIN, *in prison.*

Alm. Sleep is as nice as woman ;
The more I court it, the more it flies me.
Thy elder brother will be kinder yet :
Unsent-for death will come.   To-morrow !
Well, what can to-morrow do ?
'Twill cure the sense of honour lost ;
I and my discontents shall rest together,
What hurt is there in this ?   But death against
The will is but
A slovenly kind of potion ;
And though prescrib'd by heaven, it goes
Against men's stomachs.
So does it at fourscore too, when the soul's
Mew'd up in narrow darkness : neither sees nor hears.
Pish, 'tis mere fondness in our nature !
A certain clownish cowardice, that still
Would stay at home, and dares not venture
Into foreign countries, though better than
Its own.   Ha, what countries ? for we receive
Descriptions of th' other world from our divines,
As blind men take relation of this from us :
My thoughts lead me into the dark, and there
They'll leave me, I'll no more on it.   Within !
                                    [*Knocks.*

Enter Guard.

Alm. Some paper and a light : I'll write to th'
    king :

Defy him, and provoke a quick despatch.
I would not hold this ling'ring doubtful state
So long again, for all that hope can give.

  Enter three of the guard with paper and ink.

That sword does tempt me strangely : [*Writing.*
Were't in my hands, 'twere worth the other two.
But then the guard? it sleeps or drinks ; maybe
To contrive it so that if I should not pass,—
Why, if I fall in't, 'tis better yet than pageantry—
    [*One of the guard peeps over his shoulder.*
A scaffold and spectators ; more soldier-like—
Uncivil villain, read my letter ! [*Seizes his sword.*
 1 *Guard.* Not I, not I, my lord.
 Alm. Deny it too?
 Guard. Murder, murder !
 Guard. Arm, arm !   [*The guard runs out.*
 Alm. I'll follow, give the alarm with them.
'Tis least suspicious. Arm, arm, arm !

  Enter Soldiers, *running over the stage, one throwing
    away his arms.*

 All. The enemy, the enemy !
 Sol. Let them come, let them come, let them
  come !
    Enter ALMERIN.

 Alm. I hear fresh noise,
The camp's in great disorder : where am I now?
'Tis strangely dark. Goddess without eyes,
Be thou my guide, for blindness and sight
Are equal sense, of equal use, this night. [*Exit.*

  Enter GRAINEVERT, STRATHEMAN, VILLANOR,
    MARINEL.

 Gra. Trouble not thyself, child of discontent :
'Twill take no hurt, I warrant thee ; the State

Is but a little drunk, and when it has spew'd
Up that that made it so, it will
Be well again—there's my opinion in short.

Mar. 'Th' art i' th' right.   The State is a pretty
Forehanded State, and will do reason hereafter.
Let's drink, and talk no more on't.

All. A good motion, a good motion!
Let's drink.

Vil. Ay, ay, let's drink again.

Str. Come, to a mistress!

Gra. Agreed.
Name, name.

Vil. Anybody.   Vermilia.

Gra. Away with it.

> *She's pretty to walk with,*
> *And witty to talk with,*
> *And pleasant too to think on:*
> *But the best use of all*
> *Is, her health is a stale*
> *And helps us to make us drink on.*

Str. Excellent.   Gentlemen, if you say the word,
We'll vaunt credit, and affect high pleasure;
Shall we?

Vil. Ay, ay, let's do that.

Str. What think ye of the sacrifice now?

Mar. Come, we'll ha't; for trickling tears are
vain.

Vil. The sacrifice? what's that?

Str. Child of ignorance, 'tis a camp-health.
An *à-la-mode* one.   Grainevert, begin it.

Gra. Come, give it me.
Let me see   [*Pins up a rose.*
Which of them this rose will serve.
Hum, hum, hum!

> *Bright star o' th' lower orb, twinkling inviter,*
> *Which draw'st, as well as eyes, but sett'st men righter:*

For who at thee begins, comes to the place,
Sooner than he that sets out at the face :
Eyes are seducing lights, that the good women know,
And hang out these a nearer way to show.

Mar. Fine and pathetical! Come, Villanor.
Vil. What's the matter ?
Mar. Come, your liquor and your stanzas :
Lines, lines !
 Vil. Of what?
 Mar. Why, of anything your mistress has given
  you.
 Vil. Gentlemen, she never gave me anything but a
  box
O' th' ear for offering to kiss her once.
 Str. Of that box then.
 Mar. Ay, ay, that box, of that box !
 Vil. Since it must be,
Give me the poison then.   [*Drinks and spits.*

That box, fair mistress, which thou gav'st to me,
In human guess is like to cost me three,
Three cups of wine and verses six,
The wine will down, but verse for rhyme still sticks,
By which you all may easily, gentles, know,
I am a better drinker than a Po—

Enter DORAN.

Mar. Doran.
Gra.   *A hall, a hall*
   To welcome our friend :
   For some liquor call,
   A new or fresh face
   Must not alter our pace,
  But make us still drink the quicker :
   Wine, wine, O, 'tis divine

Come, fill it unto our brother :
What's at the tongue's end,
It forth does send,
And will not a syllable smother.
                                        Then

It unlocks the breast,
And throws out the rest,
And learns us to know each other.
        Wine! wine!

Dor. Mad lads, have you been here ever since ?
Str. Yes, faith, thou seest the worst of us.
We debauch in discipline
Four-and-twenty hours is the time.
Baruthen had the watch to-night :
To-morrow 'twill be at my tent.
Dor. Good.
And d'you know what has fall'n out to-night?
Str. Yes :
Grainevert and my Lieutenant-Colonel :
But they are friends again.
Dor. Pish, pish ! The young Palatine of Florence
And his grave guardian [were] surpris'd to-night,
    [And] carried by the enemy out of his quarters.
Gra. As a chicken by a kite out of a back-side,
Was't not so ?
Dor. Is that all?
Gra. Yes.
My Colonel did not love him :
He eats sweetmeats upon a march too.
Dor. Well—hark ye—worse yet ; Almerin's gone !
Forced the court of guard, where he was a prisoner,
And has made an escape.
Gra. So pale and spiritless a wretch
Drew Priam's curtain in the dead of night,
And told him half his Troy was burnt.   He was
Of my mind.   I would have done so myself.
Dor. Well.   There is high suspicions abroad ;

Ye shall see strange discoveries i' the council
Of war.
    Gra. What council?
    Dor. One called this morning.
Ye are all sent to.
    Gra. I will put on clean linen, and speak wisely.
    Vil. 'Sfoot, we'll have a round first.
    Gar. By all means, sir.

Sings.

> *Come, let the State stay,*
>   *And drink away:*
> *There is no business above it:*
>   *It warms the cold brain,*
>   *Makes us speak in high strain;*
> *He's a fool that does not approve it.*
>   *The Macedon youth*
>   *Left behind him this truth,*
> *That nothing is done with much thinking;*
>   *He drank and he fought,*
>   *Till he had what he sought,*
> *The world was his own by good drinking.* [*Exeunt.*

Enter GENERAL OF THE REBELS, PALATINE OF TORK,
PALATINE OF MENSECK, FRANCELIA, ALMERIN,
MORAT, IPHIGENE [*disguised*].

    Gen. As your friend, my lord, he has the privilege
Of ours, and may enjoy a liberty we would
Deny to enemies.
    Alm. I thank your excellence.
O Iphigene, he does not know, that thou
The nobler part of friendship hold'st,
And dost oblige, whilst I can but acknowledge.
    Men. Opportunity to statesmen is as the just degree
Of heat to chemists: it perfects all the work—
And in this pris'ner 'tis offered.
We now are there, where men should still begin:

To treat upon advantage,
The Palatine of Tork and Menseck,
With Almerin, shall to the king;
Petitions shall be drawn,
Humble in form, but such for matter,
As the bold Macedonian youth would send
To men he did despise for luxury.
The first begets opinion of the world,
Which looks not far, but on the outside dwells:
Th' other enforces courage in our own,
For bold demands must boldly be maintained.

Pal. Let all go on still in the public name,
But keep an ear open to particular offers;
Liberty and public good are like great aloes—
Must have the upper end still of our tables,
Though they are but for show.

Fran. Would I
Had never seen this shape, 't has poison in't,
Yet where dwells good, if ill inhabits there?

Mens. Press much religion,
For though we dress the scruples for the multitude,
And for ourselves reserve th' advantages
(It being much pretext), yet it is necessary;
For things of faith are so abstruse and nice,
They will admit dispute eternally.
So howsoe'er other demands appear,
These never can be proved unreasonable:
The subject being of so fine a nature,
It not submits itself to sense, but 'scapes
The trials which conclude all common doubts.

Fran. My lord, you use me as ill painters paint,
Who, while they labour to make faces fair,
Neglect to make them like.

Iph. Madam, there is no shipwreck of your
Virtues near, that you should throw away
Any of all your excellences
To save the dearest, modesty.

Gen. If they proceed with us, we can retreat
Unto our expositions and the people's votes.
If they refuse us wholly, then we plead,
The king's besieged, block'd up so straitly
By some few, [that] relief can find no way
To enter to the king, or to get out to us.
Exclaim against it loud,
Till the Polonians think it high injustice, ⋍
And wish us better yet.
Then easily do we rise unto our ends,
And will become their envy through their pity.
At worst you may confirm our party there,
Increase it too : there is one Brennoralt;
Men call him gallant, but a discontent;
My cousin, the king, hath us'd him ill;
[And] him a handsome whisper will draw.
The afternoon shall perfect what we have
Loosely now resolved.
    Iph.   If in discourse of beauty
(So large an empire) I do wander,
It will become your goodness, madam,   [*To Fran.*
To set me right; and in a country,
Where you yourself is queen,
Not suffer strangers lose themselves.
    Gen. What, making revenge, Palatine?
And taking prisoners fair ladies' hearts?
    Iph. Yes, my lord.
And have no better fortune in this war,
Than in the other; for while I think to take,
I am surprised myself.
    Fran. Dissembler, would thou wert.   [*Aside.*
    Mens. You are a courtier, my lord;
The Palatine of Florence, Almerin,
Will grace the hymeneals;
And that they may be, while his stay is here,
I'll court my lord in absence; take off for you

The little strangenesses virgins wear at first,
Look to the Palatine !¹   [*Iphigene swoons.*
   Mor. How is't, my dearest Iphigene?   [*Aside.*
 Iph. Not well, I would retire.
   Gen. A qualm.
   Lord. His colour stole away ; sank down, as water
In a weather-glass pressed by a warm hand.

Enter a Trumpet *blinded.*

   Mens. A cordial of kind looks from the king.
   Mor. Let us withdraw, and hear him.   [*Exit.*

Enter BRENNORALT, DORAN, RAGUELIN.

   Dor. Yes, to be married !
What, are you mute now?
   Bren. Thou cam'st too hastily upon me, putt'st
So close the colours to mine eye, I could
Not see.   It is impossible.
   Dor.   Impossible ?
If't were impossible, it should be otherwise;
What can you imagine there of constancy ?
Where 'tis so much their nature to love change,
That when they say but what they are,
Th' excuse themselves for what they do ?
   Bren. She hardly knows him yet, in such an in-
    stant.
   Dor. O, you know not how fire flies,
When it does catch light matter, woman.
   B. No more of that.   She is yet the most precious
Thing in all my thoughts.   If it be so,
I am a lost thing in the world, Doran.   [*Studies.*
   Dor. How ?
   Bren. Thou wilt in vain persuade me to be other.

---

¹ [*i.e.,* Iphigene, who is so disguised.]

Life, which to others is a good, that they
Enjoy, to me will be an evil, I
Shall suffer in.
    Dor. Look on another face : that's present remedy.
    Bren. How ill thou dost conclude !
'Cause there are pestilent airs, which kill men sud-
    denly
In health, must there be sovereign, as suddenly
To cure in sickness ? 't never was in nature.   [*Exit.*

           He enters again hastily.

I was a fool to think death only kept
The doors of ill-paid love, when or disdain
Or spite could let me out as well !
    Dor. Right : were I as you, it should no more
    trouble me
To free myself of love than to spit out
That which made me sick.
    Bren. I'll tell her so, that she may laugh at me,
As at a prisoner threatening his guard
He will break loose, and so is made the faster.
She hath charms.   [*Studies.*
Doran can fetch in a rebellious heart, e'en while
It is conspiring liberty.   O, she hath all
The virtues of her sex, and not the vices :
Chaste and unsullied as first op'ning lilies
Or untouch'd buds.
    Dor. Chaste? why, do you honour me,
Because I throw myself not off a precipice?
'Tis her ruin to be otherwise.   Though we
Blame those that kill themselves, my lord,
We praise not him that keeps himself alive,
And deserves nothing.
    Bren.   And it is the least.
She does triumph, when she does but appear :
I have as many rivals as beholders.
    Dor. All that increases but our jealousies ;

If you have now such qualms for that you have not,
What will you have for that you shall possess?

   Bren. Dull heretic! Know I have these, because
I have not her. When I have her, I shall
Have these no more.
Her fancy now, her virtue then, will govern;
And as I use to watch with doubtful eye
The wavering needle in the best sundial,
Till it has settled, then the trouble's o'er :
Because I know, when it is fix'd, it's true :
So here my doubts are all afore me. Sure,
Doran, crown'd conquerors are but the types
Of lovers, which enjoy, and really
Possess what th' other have in dreams! I'll send
A challenge to him.

   Dor. Do, and be
Thought a madman! To what purpose?
If she love him, she will but hate you more.
Lovers in favour, Brennoralt, are gamesters
In good fortune : the more you set them,
The more they get.

   Bren. I'll see her, then,
This night ; by heavens, I will.

   Dor. Where? in the citadel?

   Bren. Know what and why?

   Dor. He raves. [*Aside.*] Brennoralt!

   Bren. Let me alone. I conjure thee, by the
Discretion left betwixt us—that is, thine ;
For mine's devour'd by injuries of fortune—
Leave me to myself.

   Dor. I have done.

   Bren. Is there such a passage as thou hast told
Me of into the castle?

   Rag. There is, my lord.

   Bren. And dar'st thou let me in?

   Rag. If you, my lord,
Will venture.

Bren. There are no sentries near it?

Rag. None.

Bren. How to the chamber afterward?

Rag. Her woman.

Bren. What's she?

Rag. A wicket to my lady's secrets,
One that stands up to marriage with me.

Bren. There! upon thy life, be secret. [*Flings a purse.*

Rag. Else all punishment to ingratitude.

Bren. Enough.
I am a storm within, O Doran! till I am there.
That that which is so pleasant to behold,
Should be such pain within!

Dor.   Poor Brennoralt!
Thou art the martyr of a thousand tyrants:
Love, honour, and ambition reign by turns,
And show their power upon thee.

Bren. Why, let them; I'm still Brennoralt.   "Ev'n
    kings
Themselves are by their servants rul'd sometimes;
Let their own slaves govern them at odd hours,
Yet not subject their persons or their powers."

[*Exeunt.*

ACTUS III.   SCŒNA I.

Enter IPHIGENE, *disguised as before, as in a garden.*

Iph. What have I got by changing place,
But as a wretch which ventures to the wars,
Seeking the misery with pain abroad,
He found, but wisely thought h' had left at home.
Fortune, thou hast no tyranny beyond
This usage. [*Weeps.*] Would I had never hop'd,
Or had betimes despair'd! let never in
The gentle thief, or kept him but a guest,
Not made him lord of all.

Tempests of wind thus (as my storms of grief
Carry my tears, which should relieve my heart)
Have hurried to the thankless ocean clouds
And showers, that needed not at all the courtesy,
When the poor plains have languish'd for the want,
And almost burnt asunder.
I'll have this statue's place, and undertake
At my own charge to keep the water full.　[*Lies down.*

Enter FRANCELIA.

　Fran. These fond impressions grow too strong upon
　　me ;
They were at first without design or end ;
Like the first elements, that know not what
And why they act, and yet produce strange things :
Poor innocent desires, journeying they know
Not whither ; but now they promise to themselves
Strange things, grow insolent, threaten
No rest till they be satisfi'd.
What difference was between these lords?
The one made love, as if he by assault
Would take my heart, so forced it to defence ;
While t'other blew it up with secret mines,
And left no place for it.　Here he is,
Tears steal, too, from his eyes,
As if not daring to be known to pass
That way.　Make it good, cunning grief,
Thou know'st thou couldst not dress thyself
In any other looks, to make thee lovely.
　　　　　　　　　　　　[*Iphigene sees her.*
　Iph. Francelia !
If through the ignorance of places
I have intruded on your privacies, found out
Forbidden paths, 'tis fit you pardon, madam :
For 'tis my melancholy, not I, offends.
　Fran. So great a melancholy would well become

Mischances, such as time could not repair.
Those of the war are but the petty cures
Of every coming hour.

    Iph. Why should I not tell her all? since 'tis in
      her
To save my life? Who knows, but she may be
Gallant so far, as to undo herself
To make another happy? [*Aside.*] Madam,
The accidents of war contribute least
To my sad thoughts (if any such I have)—
Imprisonment can never be, where the
Place holds what we must love, and yet——

    Fran. My lord?
    Iph.   In this imprisonment——
    Fran.   Proceed,
My lord.

    Iph. I dare not, madam.
    Fran. I see
I do disturb you, and enter upon secrets,
Which when I know, I cannot serve you in them.

    Iph. O, most of any! You are the cause of all.
    Fran. I, my lord?
    Iph.   You, madam, you alone!
    Fran. Alas, that 'tis too soon to understand. [*Aside.*
    Iph. Must not you marry Almerin?
    Fran.   They tell me
'Tis design'd.

    Iph. If he have you, I am for ever lost.
    Fran. Lost!
The heavens forbid they should design so ill;
Or when they shall, that I should be the cause!

    Iph. Ha! her eyes are strangely kind; she prompts
Me excellently. Stars, be propitious!
And I am safe—a way I not expected.   [*Aside.*
    Fran. His passion labours for vent.   [*Aside.*
    Iph. Is there a hope you will not give yourself
To Almerin?

Fran. My lord, this air
Is common ; the walks within are pleasanter. [*Exit.*
  Iph.   [An] invitation !
God of desires, be kind, and fill me now
With language, such thou lend'st thy favourites,
When thou wouldst give them easy victories :
And I forgive thee all thy cruelties. [*Exit after her.*

  Enter PALATINE OF TORK, MENSECK, ALMERIN,
          BRENNORALT, Lords.

  Mens. Consider, too, that those who are
Necessitated to use violence
Have first been violent by necessity.
  Pal. But still you judge not right of the prerogative;
" For oft it stands with pow'r and law,
As with our faith and reason : 'tis not all
Against that is above," my lord.
  2 *Lord.* You Lithuanians had of all least reason ;
For, would the king be unjust to you, he
Cannot, where there's so little to be had.
  Alm. Where there is least, there's liberty, my lord ;
And 'tis more injury to pull hairs from
The bald, than from the bushy heads.
                          [*They go off talking.*
  Pal.   Brennoralt, a word !
                      [*Tork pulls Brennoralt.*
My lord, the world hath cast his eye upon you,
And mark'd you out one of the foremost men.
Y' have busied fame the earliest of any,
And send her still on errands.
Much of the bravery of your nation
Has taken up its lodging in you,
And gallant men but copy from you.
  Bren. 'Tis goodly language this ; what would it
    mean ?
  Pal. The Lithuanians wish you well, and wonder
So much desert should be so ill rewarded.

Bren. Good.

Pal. While all the gifts the crown is mistress of
Are plac'd upon the empty.

Bren. Still I take you not.

Pal. Then, to be plain, our army would be proud
    of you :
Pay the neglected scores of merit double.
All that you hold here of command, and what
Your fortune in this Sigismond has suffer'd,
Repair, and make it fairer than at first.

Bren. How? than nothing?
[My] lord, [a] trifle below ill language !
How came it in thy heart to tempt my honour?

Pal. My lord?

Bren. Dost think, 'cause I am angry with
The king and state sometimes, I am
Fallen out with virtue and myself?   Draw !
Draw, or by goodness——

Pal. What means your lordship?

Bren.   Draw, I say.
He that would think me a villain, is one ;
And I do wear this toy to purge the world
Of such.

Enter KING OF POLAND, Lords, MELIDOR, MIESTA.

      They've sav'd thee.   Wert thou good-natur'd,
Thou wouldst love the king the better during life.

King. If they be just, they call for gracious answers;
Speedy, howe'er, we promise.

               [*They all kiss the King's hand.*

All. Long live great Sigismond !

Bren.   The Lithuanians, sir,
Are of the wilder sort of creatures, must
Be rid with cavezous[1] and with harsh curbs.
And since the war can only make them tried,

---

[1] [Old copies, *cavilous.*]

What can be used but swords? where men have fall'n,
From not respecting royalty, unto
A liberty of offending it : what though
Their numbers possibly equal yours, sir?
And now, forc'd by necessity, like cats
In narrow rooms, they fly up in your face.
Think you rebellion and loyalty
Are empty names? and that in subjects' hearts
They don't both give and take away the courage?
Shall we believe there is no difference
In good and bad? that there's no punishment
Or no protection? forbid it, heaven !
If when great Poland's honour—safety too,
Hangs in dispute, we should not draw our swords,
Why were we ever taught to wear 'em, sir?
   Mi. This late commotion in your kingdom, sir,
Is like a growing wen upon the face,
Which as we cannot look on but with trouble,
So take't away we cannot but with danger.
War there hath foulest face, and I most fear it,
Where the pretence is fair'st.   Religion
And liberty (most specious names) they urge ;
Which like the bills of subtle mountebanks,
Fill'd with great promises of curing all, though by
The wise pass'd by as common cosenage,
Yet by th' unknowing multitude they're still
Admir'd and flock'd unto.
   King.   Is there no way
To disabuse them?
   Mel.   All is now too late.
The vulgar in religion are like
Unknown lands ; those that first possess them have
    them.
Then, sir, consider, justness of cause is nothing,
When things are risen to the point they are ;
'Tis either not examin'd or believed among
The warlike.

The better cause the Grecians had of yore,
Yet were the gods themselves divided in't;
And the foul ravisher found as good protection
As the much-injur'd husband.
Nor are you, sir, assur'd of all behind you;
For though your person in your subjects' hearts
Stands highly honour'd and belov'd, yet are
There certain acts of state, which men call grievances,
Abroad; and though they bear them in the times
Of peace, yet will they now perchance seek to
Be free, and throw them off. " For know, dread sir,
The common people are much like the sea,
That suffers things to fall and sink unto
The bottom in a calm, which (in a storm
Stirr'd and enrag'd) it lifts, and does keep up."
Then time distempers cures more safely, sir,
Than physic does, or instant letting blood;
Religion now is a young mistress there,
For which each man will fight and die at least;
Let it alone a while, and 'twill become
A kind of married wife: people will be
Content to live with it in quietness,
If that at least may be.   My voice is therefore, sir,
For peace.
    Mens. Were, sir, the question simply war or peace,
It were no more than shortly to be ask'd,
Whether we would be well or ill; since war
The sickness of the kingdom is, and peace the health.
But here I do conceive, 'twill rather lie,
Whether we had not better endure
Sharp sickness for a time, to enjoy
A perfect strength, than have it languish on us;
For peace and war in an incestuous line
Have still begot each other.
Those men that highly now have broke all laws
(The great one only 'tis 'twixt man and man),
What safety can they promise, though you give it?

Will they not still suspect, and justly too,
That all those civil bonds new-made should be
Broken again to them? So being still
In fears and jealousies themselves, they must
Infect the people; "for in such a case
The private safety is the public trouble."
Nor will they ever want pretext; "since he
That will maintain it with his sword he's injur'd,
May say't at any time."
Then, sir, as terrible as war appears,
My vote is for't; nor shall I ever care,
How ugly my physician's face shall be,
So he can do the cure.
    Lord. In vent'ring [1] physic,
I think, sir, none so much considers
The doctor's face as his own body.
To keep on foot the war with all your wants,
Is to let blood, and take strong potions
In dangerous sickness.
    King. I see, and wonder not to find, my lords,
This difference in opinion; the subject's large:
Nor can we there too much dispute where, when
We err, 'tis at a kingdom's charges. Peace
And war are in themselves indifferent,
And time doth stamp them either good or bad,
But here the place is much considerable;
"War in our own [2] is like to too much heat
Within, it makes the body sick; when in
Another country, 'tis but exercise;
Conveys that heat abroad, and gives it health.
To that I bend my thoughts; but leave it to
Our greater council, which we now assemble:
Meantime, exchange of pris'ners only we
Assent unto.
    Lord.   Nothing of truce, sir?

---

[1] [Old copies, *entring.*]   [2] [*i.e.,* Our own country.]

King. No : we'll not take up
Quiet at int'rest : perfect peace or nothing.
" Cessations for short times in war are like
Small fits of health in desp'rate maladies :
Which, while the instant pain seems to abate,
Flatters into debauch and worse estate."   [*Exeunt.*

Enter IPHIGENE, *as leading to her chamber* FRANCELIA,
    Servants *with lights*, MORAT, *and another* Soldier.

Iph. I have not left myself a fair retreat,
And must be now the blest object of your love,
Or subject of your scorn.
    Fran. I fear some treachery ;
And that mine eyes have given intelligence.
Unless you knew there would be weak defence,
You durst not think of taking in a heart,
As soon as you sat down before it.
    Iph. Condemn my love not of such fond ambition,
It aims not at a conquest, but exchange, Francelia.
                                [*In a whisper.*
    Mor. They're very great in this short time. [*Aside.*
    Sol. 'Tis ever so.   Young and handsome
Are [1] made acquaintances in nature.
So, when they meet, they have the less to do.
It is for age or ugliness to make approaches,
And keep a distance.   [*Aside.*
    Iph. When I shall see other perfection,
Which at the best will be but other vanity,
Not more I shall not love it.
    Fran. 'Tis still one step not to despair, my lord.
            [*Exeunt Iphigene, Francelia, and Servants.*
    Mor. Dost think he will fight?
    Sol.   Troth, it may be, not.
Nature, in those fine pieces, does as painters :
Hangs out a pleasant excellence, that takes

---

[1] [Old copies, *Have.*]

The eye, which is indeed but a coarse canvas in
The naked truth, or some slight stuff.
   Mor. I have a great mind to taste him.
   Sol. Fie ! a prisoner ?
   Mor. By this hand, if I thought
He courted my colonel's mistress in earnest !

Enter IPHIGENE, *a* Waiting-woman *coming after him.*

   Wom. [*to Iph.*] My lord, my lord, my lady thinks
The jessamine walks will be the finer ;
The freshness of th' morning takes off the strength
O' th' heat, she says.
   Iph. 'Tis well.
   Mor. Mew ! do it so ?   I suspect vildly.
We'll follow him, and see if he be
So far qualified towards a soldier,
As to drink a crash in's chamber.
              [*Raguelin pulls the Waiting-woman back.*
   Rag. What are these keys ?
   Wom.   Hark you, I dare not do it.
   Rag. How?
   Wom. My lady will find——
   Rag. Scruples ?   Are my hopes become your fears ?
There was no other way I should be anything
In this lewd world, and now—
'Sfoot, I know she longs to see him too.
   Wom. Does she ?
   Rag. Do you think he would desire it else ?
   Wom. Ay, but——
   Rag. Why, let me secure it all.
I'll say I found the keys, or stole them.   Come.
   Wom. Well, if you ruin all now—
Here, these enter the garden from the works,[1]

[1 The outworks, probably, mentioned in the fourth act.]

That the privy walks, and that the back stairs.
Then you know my chamber?
    Rag. Yes, I know your chamber.   [*Exeunt.*

Enter BRENNORALT.

    Bren.   He comes not.
One wise thought more, and I return :
I cannot in this act separate the foolish
From the bold so far, but still it tastes o' th' rash.
Why, let it taste ! it tastes of love too,
And to all actions 't gives a pretty relish, that——

Enter RAGUELIN.

    Rag. My lord?
    Bren. O, here !
    Rag. 'Sfoot, you're upon our sentries ;
Move on this hand.   [*Exeunt.*

Enter again BRENNORALT *and* RAGUELIN.

    Bren.   Where are we now?
    Rag. Entering part of the fort,
Your lordship must be wet a little.   [*Exeunt.*

They enter again.

    Bren. Why, are there here no guards ?
    Rag.   There needs none :
You presently must pass a place,
Where one's an army in defence,
It is so steep and strait.
    Bren.   'Tis well.
    Rag. These are the steps of danger.   Look to your
    way,
My lord.
    Bren. I do not find such difficulty.
        [*Exit Raguelin.*

Enter Francelia, *as in a bed, asleep.*

Bren. Wait me hereabouts.   [*Draws the curtains.*
So misers look upon their gold, which while
They joy to see, they fear to lose ; the pleasure
O' the sight scarce equalling the jealousy
Of being dispossess'd by others.
Her face is like the Milky Way i' th' sky,
A meeting of gentle lights without name.
Heavens ! shall this fresh ornament
Of the world, this precious loveliness
Pass, with other common things, amongst
The wastes of time ?   What pity 'twere !
     Fran. [*waking.*] Bless me ! is it a vision, or
          Brennoralt ?
     Bren. Brennoralt, lady.
     Fran. Brennoralt ? innocence guard me ;
What is it you have done, my lord ?
     Bren.   Alas !
I were in too good estate if
I knew what I did.   But why ask you, madam ?
     Fran. It much amazes me to think how you
Came hither, and what could
Bring you t' endanger thus my honour,
And your own life !
Nothing but saving of my brother
Could make me now preserve you.
     Bren. Reproach me not the follies you yourself
Make me commit.   I am reduc'd to such extremity,
That Love himself (high tyrant as he is), if he
Could see, would pity me.
     Fran.   I understand you not.
     Bren. Would heaven you did, for 'tis a pain to tell
          you :
I come t' accuse you of injustice, madam !
You first begot my passion, and was content,
At least you seem'd so, it should live ;

Yet since would ne'er contribute unto it,
Not look upon't; as if you had desired
Its being for no other end, but for
The pleasure of its ruin.
   Fran.   Why do
You labour thus to make me guilty of
An injury to you—to you, which when it is done,[1]
All mankind is alike engag'd, and must
Have quarrel to me?
    Bren. I have done ill; you chide me justly,
      madam.
I'll lay't not on you, but on my wretched self;
For I am taught that heavenly bodies
Are not malicious in their influence,
But by the disposition of the subject.
They tell me you must marry Almerin?
Sure such excellency ought to be
The recompense of virtue, not the sacrifice
Of parents' wisdom. Should it not, madam?
    Fran. 'Twould injure me, were it thought otherwise.
    Bren. And shall he have you then, that knew you
      yesterday?
Is there in martyrdom no juster way,
But he, that holds a finger in the fire
A little time, should have the crown from them,
That have endured the flame with constancy?
    Fran. If the discovery will ease your thoughts,
My lord, know Almerin is as the man
I never saw.
    Bren.   You do not marry then?
Condemned men thus hear, and thus receive
Reprieves. One question more, and I am gone:
Is there in th'[2] latitude of eternity
A hope for Brennoralt?

---

     [1] [Old copies, *one.*]   [2] [Old copies, *to.*]

Fran. My lord?

Bren. Have I a place at all when you do think of
men?

Fran. My lord, a high one;
I must be singular, did I not value you:
The world does set great rates upon you,
And you have first deserv'd them.

Bren. Is this all?

Fran. All.

Bren. O, be less kind or kinder:
Give me more pity or more cruelty, Francelia;
I cannot live with this, nor die.

Fran. I fear, my lord, you must not hope beyond it.

Bren. Not hope? This, sure, is not the body to
[*Views himself.*
This soul; it was mistaken, shuffled in
Through haste: why else should that have so much
love,
And this want loveliness to make that love
Receiv'd? I will raise honour to a point
It never was—do things of such   [*Studies.*
A virtuous greatness she shall love me.
She shall; I will deserve her, though
I have her not. There's something yet in that.
Madam, will't please you, pardon my offence?
O Fates! that I must call thus my affection!

Fran. I will do anything, so you will think
Of me and of yourself, my lord, and how
Your stay endangers both.

Bren. Alas!
Your pardon is more necessary to
My life, than life to me. But I am gone;
Blessings, such as my wishes for you in
Their ecstasies could never reach, fall on you!
May everything contribute to preserve
That exc'llence (my destruction), till't meet joys
In love, great as the torments I have in't.   [*Exit.*

ACTUS IV.   SCŒNA I.

Enter BRENNORALT.

Bren. Why so, 'tis well.   Fortune, I thank thee
    still,
I dare not call thee villain neither.
'Twas plotted from the first, that's certain.
It looks that way !   Hum ! caught in a trap.
Here's something yet to trust to.   [*To his sword.*
This was the entry, these the stairs ;
But whither afterwards ?
He that is sure to perish on the land,
May quit the niceties of card and compass ;
And safe, to his discretion, put to sea :
He shall have my hand to't.   [*Exit.*

Enter RAGUELIN *and* ORILLA *the waiting-woman.*

Rag. Look ! by this light, 'tis day.
Ori. [No,] not by this ; by t'other 'tis indeed.
Rag. Thou art such another piece of temptation.
My lord raves by this time.   A hundred to one,
The sentinels will discover us too :
Then I do pray for night-watch !
    Ori.   Fie upon thee !
Thou art as fearful as a young colt.
Bogglest at everything, fool ?   As if
Lovers had considered hours : I'll peep in.
                            [*She retires to peep.*
    Rag. I am as weary of this wench
As if I were married to her ;
She hangs upon me like an ape upon a horse ;

She's as common, too, as a barber's glass ;
Conscienced, too, like a dye-dapper.

Ori. [*coming back.*] There's nobody within.
My lady sleeps this hour at least.

Rag. Good, the devil's even with me :
Not be an honest man neither.
What course now ?

Enter BRENNORALT *and a* Guard (*disguised*).

Sol. Nay, sir, we shall order you now.
Bren. Dogs !

Enter FRESOLIN.

Fre. What tumult's this?—ha ! Brennoralt ! 'tis he
In spite of his disguise : what makes he here?
He's lost for ever, if he be discovered ;
How now, companions, why do you use my friend thus?

Sol. Your friend, my lord? if he be your friend
He has used us ill ;
He has played the devil amongst us.
Six of our men are surgeons' work this month.
We found him climbing the walls.

2 *Sol.* He had no word [1] neither ;
Nor any language but a blow.

Fre. You will be doing these wild things, my lord,
Good faith, ye are to blame ; if y' had desir'd
To view the walls or trenches, 'twas but
Speaking : we are not nice.
I would myself have waited on you :
They're the new outworks you would see perchance.
Boy, bring me Black Tempest round about
And the grey Barbary ; [2] a trumpet come along too.
My lord, we'll take the nearer way
And privater here through the sally-port.

---

[1] [Password.]   [2] [The names of two chargers.]

Bren. What a devil is this? sure I dream.
                  [Exeunt. Soldiers remain.
Sol. Now you are so officious !
2 *Sol.* Death ! could I guess he was a friend ?
Sol. 'Twas ever to be thought ;
How should he come there else ?
  2 *Sol.* Friend or no friend, he might have left us
Something to pay the surgeon with :
Grant me that, or I'll beat you to't.   *[Exeunt.*

       Enter FRESOLIN *and* BRENNORALT.

Fre. Brennoralt, start not :
I pay thee back a life I owe thee,
And bless my stars they gave me power to do't ;
The debt lay heavy on me.
A horse waits you there, a trumpet too
(Which you may keep, lest he should prate)—
No ceremony, 'tis dangerous.
  Bren. Thou hast astonish'd me :
Thy youth hath triumphed in one single act
O'er all the age can boast ; and I will stay
To tell thee so, were they now firing all
Their cannons on me.   Farewell ! gallant Fresolin,
And may reward, great as thy virtue, crown thee.
                  [Exeunt divers ways.

       Enter IPHIGENE *and* FRANCELIA.

Fran. A peace will come, and then you must be
    gone ;
And whether, when you once are got upon the wing,
You will not stoop to what shall rise,
Before ye fly to some lure with
More temptation garnish'd, is a sad question,
  Iph. Can you have doubts, and I not fears ? [1]

---

        [1] [Old copies, *my fears.*]

By this, the readiest and the sweetest oath [*kisses her*],
    I swear
I cannot so secure myself of you ;
But in my absence I shall be in pain.
I have cast up what it will be to stand
The governor's anger ; and, which is more hard,
The love of Almerin.   I hold thee now
But by thy own free grant—a slight security !
Alas ! it may fall out, giving thyself :
Not knowing thine own worth or want of mine ;
Thou mayst, like kings deceiv'd, resume the gift
On better knowledge back.
    Fran.   If I so easily change,
I was not worth your love, and by the loss you'll gain.
    Iph. But when you're irrecoverably gone,
'Twill be slight comfort to persuade myself
You had a fault, when all that fault must be
But want of love to me ; and then [1] again
Find in my much defect so much excuse,
That it will have no worse name than discretion.
If unconcerned [you] do cast it up—
I must have more assurance.
    Fran. You have too much already ;
And sure, my lord, you wonder, while I blush,
At such a growth in young affections.
    Iph. Why should I wonder, madam ?
Love, that from two breasts sucks,
Must of a child quickly become a giant.
Dunces in love stay at the alphabet :
The inspir'd know all before ;
And do begin still higher.

           Enter Waiting-woman.

    Wom. Madam, Almerin returned has sent to kiss
Your hands.   I told him you were busy !

---

         [1] [Old copies, *that.*]

Fran. Must I, my lord, be busy?
I may be civil, though not kind.
Tell him, I wait him in the gallery.
    Iph. May I not kiss your hand this night?
                                    [*In a whisper.*
    Fran. The world is full of jealous eyes, my lord;
And were they all lock'd up, you are a spy,
Once entered in my chamber at strange hours.
    Iph. The virtue of Francelia is too safe
To need those little arts of preservation.
Thus to deny [1] ourselves, is to distrust ourselves.
A cherubin despatches not on earth
The affairs of heaven with greater innocence
Than I will visit; 'tis but to take a leave—
I beg.
    Fran. When you are going, my lord.   [*Exeunt.*

Enter ALMERIN, MORAT.

    Alm. Pish! Thou liest, thou liest.
I know he plays with womankind, not loves it.
Thou art impertinent.
    Mor. 'Tis the camp-talk, my lord, though.
    Alm. The camp's an ass; let me hear no more on't.
                                    [*Exeunt talking.*

Enter GRAINEVERT, VILLANOR, *and* MARINEL.

    Gra. And shall we have peace?
I am no sooner sober but the state is so too:
If't be thy will, a truce for a moneth only.
I long to refresh my eyes, by this hand;
They have been so tir'd with looking upon faces
Of this country.
    Vil. And shall the Donnazella
To whom we wish so well-a,
Look babies again in our eyes-a?

-----
[1] [Old copies, *divide.*]

Gra. Ah! a sprightly girl about [1] fifteen,
That melts when a man but takes her by the
    hand:
Eyes full and quick; with breath
Sweet as double violets, and wholesome
As dying leaves of strawberries.
Thick silken eyebrows, high upon the forehead;
And cheeks mingled with pale streaks of red,
Such as the blushing morning never wore.
    Vil. O my chops, my chops!
    Gra. With narrow mouth, small teeth,
And lips swelling, as if she pouted——
    Vil. Hold, hold, hold!
    Gra. Hair curling, and cover'd like buds of mar-
    joram;
Part tied in negligence, part loosely flowing——
    Mar. Tyrant, tyrant, tyrant!
    Gra. In a pink-colour raffata petticoat,
Laced smock-sleeves dangling!
This vision stolen from her own bed,
And rustling into one's chamber!
    Vil. O good Grainevert, good Grainevert!
    Gra. With a wax candle in her hand,
Looking as if she had lost her way
At twelve at night.
    Mar. O, any hour, any hour!
    Gra. Now I think on't, by this hand,
I'll marry, and be long-liv'd.
    Vil. Long-liv'd! how?
    Gra. O, he that has a wife eats with an appetite,
Has a very good stomach to't first:
This living at large is very destructive,
Variety is like rare sauces: provokes too far,
And draws on surfeits more than th' other.

---

[1] [Old copies, *above.* Perhaps we should read, *not above.*]

Enter DORAN.

Dor. So; is this a time to fool in?

Gra. What's the matter?

Dor. Draw out your choice men, and away to
Your Colonel immediately.   There's work
Towards, my boys, there's work.

Gra. Art in earnest?

Dor. By this light.

Gra. There's something in that yet.

> *This moiety*[1] *war,*
> > *Twilight,*
> *Neither night nor day:*
> > *Pox upon it!*
> *A storm is worth a thousand*
> > *Of your calm;*
> *There's more variety in it.*   [*Exeunt.*

Enter ALMERIN *and* FRANCELIA, *as talking earnestly.*

Alm. Madam, that shows the greatness of my
    passion.

Fran. The imperfection rather: jealousy's
No better sign of love, my lord, than fevers are
Of life; they show there is a being, though
Impair'd and perishing: and that, affection,
But sick and in disorder.   I like't not.
Your servant.   [*Exit.*

Alm. So short and sour? the change is visible.

Enter IPHIGENE.

Iph. Dear Almerin, welcome, y' have been absent
    long.

Alm. Not very long.

Iph. To me it hath appear'd so;
What says our camp? am I not blamed there?

Alm. They wonder——

---

[1] [Half-and-half.]

Iph. While we smile?
How have you found the king inclining?
   Alm. Well.
The treaty is not broken, nor holds it.
Things are where they were;
'T has a kind of face of peace;
You, my lord, may, when you please, return.
   Iph. I, Almerin?
   Alm. Yes, my lord, I'll give you an escape.
   Iph. 'Tis least in my desires.
   Alm. Hum!
   Iph. Such prisons are beyond all liberty.
   Alm. Is't possible?
   Iph. Seems it strange to you?
   Alm. No, not at all.
What, you find the ladies kind?
   Iph. Civil.   [*Smiles.*
   Alm. You make love well too, they say, my lord.
   Iph. Pass my time.
   Alm. Address unto Francelia?
   Iph. Visit her.
   Alm. D'you know she is my mistress, Palatine?
   Iph. Ha?
   Alm. D'you know she is my mistress?
   Iph. I have been told so.
   Alm. And do you court her then?
   Iph. Why, if you saw the enemy first,
Would you not charge?   [*Smiles.*
   Alm. He does allow it too, by heaven:
Laughs at me too. Thou filcher of a heart,   [*Aside.*
False as thy title to Francelia,
Or as thy friendship: which with this I do   [*Dreams.*
Throw by. Draw!
   Iph. What do you mean?
   Alm. I see the cunning now of all thy love,
And why thou cam'st so timely kind,
Suffering surprise. Draw!

Iph. I will not draw, kill me ;
And I shall have no trouble in my death,
Knowing it is your pleasure :
As I shall have no pleasure in my life,
Knowing it is your trouble.
    Alm. O, poor —— I look'd for this.
I knew th' wouldst find 'twas easier to do a wrong
Than justify it. But——
    Iph. I will not fight ; hear me,
If I love you not more than I love her ;
If I do love her more than for your sake,
Heaven strangely punish me.
    Alm. Take heed how thou dost play with heaven.
    Iph. By all that's just, and fair, and good,
By all that you hold dear, and men hold great,
I never had lascivious thought, or e'er
Did action that might call in doubt my love
To Almerin.
    Alm. That tongue can charm me into anything ;
I do believe't : pr'ythee, be wiser then.
Give me no further cause of jealousy ;
Hurt not mine honour more, and I am well.
    Iph. But well ?   Of all
Our passions, I wonder nature made
The worst, foul jealousy, her favourite.
And if it be not so, why took she care,
That everything should give the monster nourishment,
And left us nothing to destroy it with ?
    Alm. Pr'ythee, no more ; thou plead'st so cunningly,
I fear I shall be made the guilty,
And need thy pardon.
    Iph. If you could read my heart, you would.
I will be gone to-morrow, if that will satisfy.
Indeed I shall not rest until my innocence
Be made as plain as objects to the sense.
    Alm. Come,
You shall not go, I'll think on it no more.

" Distrusts ruin not friendship,
But build it fairer than it was before."   [*Exeunt.*

Enter BRENNORALT, Captains, STRATHEMAN,
DORAN.

Bren. No more but ten from every company;
For many hands are thieves, and rob the glory,
While they take their share. How goes the night?

Str. Half spent, my lord; we shall have straight
The moon's[1] weaker light.

Bren. It is time, then; call in the officers.

Enter Officers.

Friends, if you were men that must be talk'd into
A courage, I had not chosen you;
Danger with its vizard oft before this time
Y' have look'd upon, and outfac'd it too;
We are to do the trick again—that's all.
Here——   [*Draws his sword.*
And yet we will not swear:
For he that shrinks in such an action,
Is damn'd without the help of perjury.
Doran, if from the virgin-tow'r thou spiest
A flame, such as the east sends forth about
The time the day should break, go tell the king
I hold the castle for him; bid him come on
With all his force, and he shall find a victory
So cheap, 'twill lose the value. If I fall,
The world has lost a thing it used not well;
And I, a thing I car'd not for—that world.   *i*

Str. Lead us on, Colonel;
If we do not fight like——

Bren.   No like.
We'll be ourselves' similitude,
And time shall say, when it would tell
That men did well, they fought like us.

---

[1] [To be pronounced as a dissyllable.]

ACTUS V. SCŒNA I.

Enter again.

Bren. What made thee stop?
Str. One in his falling sickness had a fit
Which choked the passage; but all is well:
Softly, we are near the place.   [*Exeunt.*

Alarm within, and fight; then enter ALMERIN
in his nightgown.

Alm. What noise is here to-night?
Something on fire? What, ho! Send to
The virgin-tower, there is disorder thereabouts.

Enter Soldiers.

Sol. All's lost, all's lost! The enemy's
Upon the place of arms; and is by this
Time master of that and the tower.
Alm. Thou liest!   [*Strikes him.*

Enter MORAT.

Mor. Save yourself, my lord, and haste unto the
     camp;
Ruin gets in on every side.
Alm. There's something in it, when this fellow flies.
Villains, my arms; I'll see what devil reigns. [*Exeunt.*

Enter IPHIGENE *and* FRANCELIA.

Iph. Look, the day breaks.
Fran. You think I'll be so kind as swear
It does not now? Indeed, I will not.
Iph. Will you not send me neither
Your picture, when y' are gone?
That when my eye is famish'd for a look,
It may have where to feed;
And to the painted feast invite my heart.

Fran. Here, take this virgin bracelet off my hair,
And if like other men thou shalt hereafter
Throw it with negligence amongst the records
Of thy weak female conquests : laugh
At the kind words and mystical contrivement :
If such a time shall come,
Know I am sighing then thy absence, Iphigene,
And weeping o'er the false but pleasing image.

Enter ALMERIN.

Alm. Francelia, Francelia,
Rise, rise, and save thyself ! the enemy
That does not know thy worth, may else destroy it.
                                     [*Throws open the door.*
Ha ! mine eyes grow sick : a plague
Has through them stol'n into my heart ;
And I grow dizzy ! Feet, lead me off again,
Without the knowledge of my body :
I shall act, I know not, what else.   [*Exit.*
    Fran. How came he in ? Dear Iphigene,
We are betray'd ! let's raise the castle, lest
He should return.
    Iph. That were to make all public. Fear not ;
I'll satisfy his anger : I can do it.
    Fran. Yes, with some quarrel !
And bring my honour and my love in danger.

Enter ALMERIN.

Look, he returns, and wrecks of fury,
Like hurried clouds over the face of heaven
Before a tempest, in his looks appear.
    Alm. If they would question what our rage doth
      act,
And make it sin, they would not thus provoke men.
I am too tame. For, if they live,
I shall be pointed at. Here I denounce a war
To all the world, and thus begin it. [*Runs at Iphigene.*

Iph. What hast thou done?   [*Falls.*
Fran. Ah me, help, help!
                              [*Almerin wounds Francelia.*
Iph. Hold!
Alm.   'Tis too late.
Iph. My fond deceits involve the innocent;
Rather than she shall suffer,[1]
I will discover all.   [*Aside.*
Alm.   Ha! what will he discover?
Iph. That which shall make thee curse
The blindness of thy rage—I am a woman!
Alm. Ha, ha, ha! brave and bold!
Because thy perjury deceived me once,
And sav'd thy life, thou think'st to escape again.
Impostor, thus thou shalt——   [*Runs at him.*
Iph. O, hold! I have enough.
Had I hope of life, thou shouldst not have this
    secret.
Fran. What will it be now?
Iph. My father having long desir'd
A son to heir his great possessions,
And in six births successively deceived,
Made a rash vow—O, how rash vows are punished!—
That if the burthen then my mother went with
Prov'd not a male, he ne'er would know her more.
Then was unhappy Iphigene brought forth,
And by the women's kindness nam'd a boy;
And since so bred—a cruel pity, as
It hath fallen out.   If now thou find'st that, which
Thou thought'st a friendship in me, love, forget it.
It was my joy—and—death.   [*Faints.*
Alm. For curiosity I'll save thee, if

---

[1] [This and the preceding line have been transposed, and the
sense has apparently by that means been made clearer. If the
text had been suffered to remain as it is in the old copies, we
must have printed the former line parenthetically.]

I can, and know the end.
If't be but loss of blood—breasts?
By all that's good, a woman! Iphigene!

Iph. I thank thee, for I was fallen asleep before
I had despatch'd. Sweetest of all thy sex,
Francelia, forgive me now; my love
Unto this man, and fear to lose him, taught me
A fatal cunning, made me court you and
My own destruction.

    Fran.   I am amaz'd.

    Alm. And can it be, O mockery of heaven!
To let me see what my soul often wish'd,
And make't my punishment—a punishment
That, were I old in sins, were yet too great?

    Iph. Would you have lov'd me, then? Pray, say
      you would:
For I, like testy sick men at their death,
Would know no news but health from the physician.

    Alm. Canst thou doubt that,
That hast so often seen me ecstasi'd
When thou wert dress'd like woman,
Unwilling ever to believe thee man?

    Iph. I have enough.

    Alm. Heavens! what thing
Shall I appear unto the world? Here might
My ignorance find some excuse, but there
I was distracted. None, but one enrag'd
With anger to a savageness, would e'er
Have drawn a sword upon such gentle sweetness.
Be kind, and kill me—kill me, one of you!
Kill me, if't be but to preserve my wits.
Dear Iphigene, take thy revenge, it will
Not misbecome thy sex at all; for 'tis
An act of pity, not of cruelty,
Thus to despatch a miserable man.

    Fran. And thou wouldst be more miserable yet,
While, like a bird made prisoner by itself,

Thou beat'st and beat'st thyself 'gainst everything,
And dost pass by that which should let thee out.
    Alm. Is it my fault, or heaven's?
Fortune, when she would play upon me,
Like ill musicians, wound me up so high,
That I must crack sooner than move in tune.
    Fran. Still you rave ; while we for want
Of present help may perish.
    Alm.   Right.
A surgeon !   I'll go find one instantly.
The enemy too !—I had forgot !
O, what fatality govern'd this night !   [*Exit.*
    Fran. How like an unthrift's case will mine be
      now?
For all the wealth he loses shifts but's place ;
And still the world enjoys it : and so will you,
Sweet Iphigene, though I possess you not.
    Iph. What excellence of nature's this !   Have you
So perfectly forgiven already, as to
Consider me a loss ?   I doubt which sex
I shall be happier in.   Climates of friendship
Are not less pleasant, 'cause they are less scorching,
Than those of love ; and under them we'll live :
Such precious links of that we'll tie our souls
Together with, that the chains of the other
Shall be gross fetters to it.
    Fran.   But I fear
I cannot stay the making.   O, would you
Had never undeceiv'd me, for I'd died with
Pleasure, believing I had been your martyr.
Now——
    Iph. She looks pale !   Francelia !
    Fran.   I cannot stay ;
A hasty summons hurries me away :
And—gives—no——   [*Dies.*
    Iph.   She's gone, she's gone !
Life, like a dial's hand, hath stol'n

From the fair figure, ere it was perceiv'd.
> [*A noise within.   Enter Soldiers.*
> *She thinks them Almerin.*

What will become of me?   Too late, too late
Y' are come ; you may persuade wild birds, that wing
The air, into a cage, as soon as call
Her wand'ring spirits back.   Ha !
Those are strange faces : there's a horror in them ;
And if I stay, I shall be taken for
The murderer.   O, in what straits they move,
That wander 'twixt death, fears, and hopes of love.
> [*Exit.*

Enter BRENNORALT, GRAINEVERT, Soldiers.

Bren. Forbear, upon your lives, the place.   There
dwells
Divinity within it.   All else the castle holds
Is lawful prize, your valour's wages.
This I claim as mine ; guard you the door.
Gra. Coronel, shall you use all the women your-
self?
Bren. Away ! it is unseasonable.
> [*Draws the curtain.*

Awake, fair saint, and bless thy poor idolater.
Ha ! pale?   And cold?   [And] dead?
The sweetest guest fled ; murdered, by heaven !
The purple streams not dry yet !
Some villain has broke in before me,
Robb'd all my hopes ; but I will find him out,
And kick his soul to hell.
I'll do it.   [*Dragging out Iphigene.*]   Speak !
Iph. What should I say?
Bren. Speak, or by all——
Iph. Alas ! I do confess
Myself th' unfortunate cause.
Bren.   O, d'you so?
Hadst thou been cause of all the plagues that vex

Mankind, thou'dst been an innocent to what
Thou art; thou shalt not think repentance. [*Kills her.*
   Iph. O, thou wert too sudden, and—— [*Dies.*
   Bren. Was I so?
The lustful youth would sure have spoil'd her honour:
Which finding highly guarded, rage and fear
To be reveal'd counsell'd this villany.
Is there no more of them? [*Exeunt.*

Enter ALMERIN.

   Alm. Not enter? Yes, dog, through thee! Ha!
A corpse laid out, instead of Iphigene!
Francelia dead too! Where shall I begin to curse?

Enter BRENNORALT.

   Bren. Here, if he were thy friend!
   Alm. Brennoralt!
A gallant sword could ne'er have come
In better time.
   Bren. I have a good one for thee,
If that will serve the turn.
   Alm. I long to try it.
That sight doth make me desperate:
Sick of myself and the world.
   Bren. Didst value him?
A greater villain did I never kill.
   Alm. Kill?
   Bren. Yes.
   Alm. Art sure of it?
   Bren. Maybe, I do not wake.
   Alm. Thou'st taken then a guilt off from me,
Would have weigh'd down my sword:
Weakened me too low [for] resistance.
I should have made no sports, hadst thou conceal'd it.
Know, Brennoralt, thy sword is stain'd in excellence,
Great as the world could boast.
   Bren. Ha, ha! how thou'rt abus'd!

Look there, there lies the excellence
Thou speak'st of! Murdered : by him too :
He did confess he was the cause.
    Alm. O innocence ill understood, and much worse
        us'd!
She was, alas! by accident; but I—
I was the cause in deed.
    Bren. I will believe thee too, and kill thee :
Destroy all causes, till I make a stop
In nature ; for to what purpose should she
Work again?
    Alm. Bravely then ;
The title of a kingdom is a trifle
To our quarrel, sir. Know by sad mistake
I kill'd thy mistress, Brennoralt,
And thou kill'dst mine.
    Bren.   Thine?
    Alm.   Yes, that Iphigene,
Though shown as man unto the world,
Was woman, excellent woman !
    Bren. I understand no riddles ; guard thee.
                         [*Fight and pause.*
    Alm. O, could they now look down, and see,
How we two strive, which first should give revenge,
They would forgive us something of the crime.
Hold ! pr'ythee, give me leave
To satisfy a curiosity—
I never kissed my Iphigene as woman.
    Bren. Thou motion'st well, nor have I taken leave.
It keeps a sweetness yet, as 'stils from roses,
When the flowers are gone.   [*Rises.*
    Alm. Even so have two faint pilgrims, scorch'd
        with heat,
Unto some neighbour fountain stepp'd aside,
Kneel'd first, then laid their warm lips to the nymph,
And from her coldness took fresh life again,
As we do now.

Bren. Let's on our journey, if thou art refresh'd.
Alm. [I] come, and if there be a place reserved
For height'ned spirits better than other,
May that which wearies first of ours have it.

               [Fight a good while; Almerin falls.

Bren. If I grow weary, laugh at me, that's all.
Alm. Brave souls above, which will be, sure,
Inquisitive for news from earth,
Shall get no other but that thou art brave.

Enter KING, STRATHEMAN, Lords, MENSECK.

King. Still gallant, Brennoralt? thy sword not
    sheath'd yet?
Busy still?
Str.   To preserve some ladies, as we guess'd.[1]
Bren. Revenging, sir,
The foulest murder ever blasted ears :
Committed here by Almerin and Iphigene !
Alm. [*reviving.*] False, false ! the first-created purity
Was not more innocent than Iphigene.
Bren. Lives he again?
Alm. Stay, thou much-wearied guest,
Till I have thrown a truth amongst them :
We shall look black else to posterity.
King. What says he?
Lord.   Something
Concerning this he labours to discover.
Alm. Know, it was I that kill'd Francelia—
I alone!
Mens. O barbarous return of my civilities.
Was it thy hand?

---

[1] [Old copies read—
    " *Str.* To preserve some ladies, as we guess'd.
     King. Still gallant, Brennoralt? thy sword not sheath'd yet?
  Busy still?"]

Alm.   Hear and forgive me, Menseck.
Entering this morning hastily,
With resolution to preserve
The fair Francelia, I found a thief
Stealing the treasure (as I thought)
Belong'd to me.   Wild in my mind,
As ruin'd in my honour, in much mistaken rage
I wounded both.   Then (O, too late!) I found
My error : found Iphigene a woman,
Acting [a] stol'n love, to make her own love safe,
And all my jealousies impossible.
Whilst I ran out to bring them cure,
Francelia dies, and Iphigene found here ;
I can no more.   [*Dies.*
    King. Most strange and intricate !
Iphigene a woman ?
    Mel. With this story I am guiltily acquainted,
The first concealments, since her love,
And all the ways to it, I have been trusted with ;
But, sir, my grief, join'd with the instant business,
Begs a deferment.
    King. I am amaz'd, till I do hear it out.
But, i' th' meantime,
Lest in these mists merit should lose itself,
Those forfeitures of Tork and Menseck,
Brennoralt, are thine.
    Bren. A princely gift !   But, sir, it comes too late.
Like sunbeams on the blasted blossoms, do
Your favours fall : you should have given me this,
When't might have rais'd me in men's thoughts, and
        made
Me equal to Francelia's love.   I have
No end, since she is not.
Back to my private life I will return.
Cattle, though weary, can trudge homewards after.
    King. This melancholy time must cure.   Come,
        take

The bodies up, and lead the prisoners on ;
Triumph and funerals must walk together,
Cypress and laurel twin'd make up one chaplet.
For we have got
The day ; but bought it at so dear a rate,
The victory itself's unfortunate.   [*Exeunt.*

FINIS.

THE SAD ONE.

The Sad One.   A Tragedy.   By Sr John Suckling.

Not in the editions of 1646 and 1648.

TO THE READER.[1]

——— o ———

I HOPE I shall not need to crave your pardon for
publishing this dramatic piece of Sir John Suckling
—imperfect, I cannot say, but rather unfinished—there
being a kind of perfection even in the most deficient
fragments of this incomparable author. To evince that
this copy was a faithful transcript from his own handwriting, I have said enough in my former epistle,[2] and
I thought it much better to send it into the world in the
same state I found it, without the least addition, than
procure it [to be] supplied by any other pen, which had
not been less preposterous than the finishing of Venus'
picture, so skilfully begun by Apelles, by some other hand.
Nor are we without a sufficient precedent in works of
this nature, and relating to an author, who confessedly
is reputed the glory of the English stage, whereby you'll
know I mean Ben Jonson, and in a play also of some-

---

[1] This preface, which can refer only to "The Sad One," is
improperly placed, in the copy of 1658 here employed, before
the Poems.   In another copy, which appears quite complete,
it is not found at all.

[2] See the Prefaces printed at the beginning of the volume.

what resembling name, "The Sad Shepherd," extant in his third volume, which, though it wants two entire Acts, was nevertheless judged a piece of too much worth to be laid aside by the learned and honourable Sir Kenelm Digby, who published that volume. We have also in print, written by the same hand, the very beginning only (for it amounts not to one full scene) of a tragedy called "Mortimer;" so that we find the same fate to have happened to the works of two of the most celebrated and happy wits of this nation. Now, as it is to have been wished that this tragedy had come whole and complete to public view, so is it some happiness that there is so much of it preserved; it being true of our author what Dr Donne said of a famous artist of his time—

"A hand or eye
By Hilliard drawn, is worth a history
By a worse painter made."

I shall add no more, but only say (with some just confidence), that I could not have answered myself to the world if I had suppressed this tragedy, and therefore may hope for some favour by its publication. Farewell.

H. M.[1]

---

[1] Humphrey Moseley.

THE ARGUMENT INTRODUCING TO THE
FOLLOWING SCENES.

———o———

SICILY had been a long time tormented with civil
wars, and the crown was still in dispute, till Aldebrand, getting the upper hand in a set battle, established
himself on the throne, and gave a period to all those
troubles in show only, for the old factions were set on
foot again shortly after, and the house of the Floretti and
the Cleonaxes strove now as much who should be most
powerful with the king, as before who should make him.
In conclusion, the favour of Aldebrand inclining to the
Cleonaxes, and by degrees resting wholly upon them,
the Floretti took arms, but in a set field lost all. The
father and the son being both taken prisoners, the one was
banish'd, the other condemned suddenly to lose his head.

Thus far the author drew the curtain ; the rest of the
plot is wrapp'd up in the following scenes.

THE ACTORS.

———o———

ALDEBRAND, King of Sicily.
CLEONAX, senior, his treasurer.
CLEONAX, junior, son of the former.
BELLAMINO, favourite of pleasure, and cousin to Cleonax.
CLARIMONT, an old lord.
CLARIMONT, junior, his son.
FIDELIO, friend to Clarimont.
FLORELIO, a lord married to Francelia.
FLORELIO, junior, his brother.
LORENZO, an ambitious courtier.
PARMENIO, his supposed creature.
DROLLIO, } two courtiers.
LEPIDO, }
DOCO DISCOPIO, one that pretends to be a great statesman.
SIGNOR MULTECARNI, the poet.
PETRUCHIO, servant to Florelio.
Ambassador from Spain.
Actors.
AMASIA, queen to Aldebrand.
FRANCELIA, daughter to Clarimont.
Keeper.

THE SCENE, SICILY.

The Sad One.

——o——

ACTUS I. SCŒNA I.

Enter old CLARIMONT *in prison, in his nightgown ;
his servant following him.*

CONDEMN'D unheard ! Just heavens, it cannot
be :
Why, tyranny itself could do no more ;
The pale ghosts of Tiberius and Nero
Would blush to see an act so foul and horrid,
So full of black ingratitude as this !
'Twas I that set the crown upon his head ;
And bad him live king of his enemies,
When he durst hardly hope it :
And does he thus requite me ? Now I see,
Who by the compass of his merit fails,
May guide his fraught of hopes in seasons fair
And calm ; but when storms come,
All his good deeds (with his good days) must perish.
O my unhappy stars !   [*Beats his breast.*

[*Enter a* Servant.]

Ser. My lord, let not a fruitless passion
Make you to die less man than you have lived.
  Clar. Who art thou ?
  Ser. I was lately one, my lord,
Of the vast crowd that waited on your fortunes,
But am now become the whole train ;
The rest have left you.
  Clar. Pr'ythee, do thou leave me too. [*Servant exit.*
The clap o' th' vulgar and loud popular applause
Are not the echo of our acts, but fortunes.
Great men but dials are, which, when the sun
Is gone or hides his face, are hardly look'd upon.
But yesterday I was time's minister ;
On me the whole court gaz'd, as at
Some comet set in Cassiopeia's chair : [1]
Who but old Clarimont could with nods create,
And with a speaking eye command bare heads and
    knees ;
But now !   [*Beats his breast again.*
Greatness is but the shadow of the beams
Of princes' favours, nourish'd in extremes ;
First taught to creep, and feed on hopes, to live
Upon the glance, and humbly to observe
Each under-minion, till its own desire
Work itself near enough to set itself on fire.
                         [*Studies a little.*
Fain would I make my audit up with heaven,
For 'tis a large one ; but the small, vain hopes,
Which yet I have of life and of revenge,
Smother these thoughts within me
Faster than they are born.

      Enter FIDELIO *disguised like a friar.*
A ghostly father ?
My minutes are but few, I see by this.

_____
      [1] [See Lovelace's Works, 1864, p. 185, note.]

Sir, you are welcome :
I was but now considering how to die,
And (trust me) I do find it something hard.
I shall extremely need some such good help
As yours to do it well.
    Fid. Faith, my lord, divines do hold
The way to die well is to live well first.
                                    [*Discovers himself.*
    Clar. Fidelio?
    Fid. Not too loud, there is danger in it.
The king has promised life ; but none as yet
Must know't ; the enemies are too potent,
And must be softened by degrees.
    Clar. Why, then, I see he hath not quite forgot
Pass'd services.
    Fid. Not too much of that :
This is not gratitude ; or, if it be, it does,
As thankfulness in great ones used to do,
It looks asquint, and seems to turn to favours,
But regards new ends.
    Clar. Pr'ythee, unriddle.
    Fid. Why, to be short, it is your daughter's beauty,
Not your merit.
    Clar. My fears prompt me too quick ;
She's not turned whore, is she?
    Fid. No ; but her honesty is so strait beset,
That, if she be not victualled well within,
And have some sudden succours,
She will, I fear, ere long surrender.
    Clar. O Fidelio, when kings do tempt,
They'd need be angels that endure the shock,
Not women.
    Fid. 'Tis true, my lord ; yet
Let not uncertain fears create new griefs :
Doubt is of all the sharpest passion,
And often turns distempers to diseases.
Collect yourself, and be assur'd my zeal

Shall watch abroad ; and when I may reveal
Myself your servant, I'll not do't in breath,
But with the adventure of my life or death.
 Clar. O, you are noble, sir, I know't,
And mean to hope the best. Farewell.   [*Exeunt.*

Enter LORENZO *and his father, with servants,
whispering together and frowning—pass over the stage.*
           [*Exeunt.*

Enter LORENZO *solus, as going to prison.*

Arm'd with the love of sovereignty and revenge,
I'll ravish fortune, and all engines try,
That heaven or hell have yet discovered ;
But I will scale my end, and plant desire
As high as any thought durst e'er aspire.
The dotage of the king shall not
Secure thee, poor old man !
Clarimont, I come ; this night our quarrel ends ;
Nothing but death could ever make us friends.
       [*Knocks at the prison door.*

Enter the Keeper.

Where's old Clarimont ?
 Keep. In's bed, my lord.
 Lor. In's grave, thou wouldst have said.
 Keep. Must he then die to-night ?
 Lor. The king will have it so ;
He fears the people love him, and to save
His life may prove tumultuous.
 Keep. Poor gentleman ! how quick is fate come
  on him !
How sudden is all woe !
Bad days have wings, the good on crutches go.
My lord, wilt please you

[To] walk into that private chamber?
The executioner shall straight be here.

> [*Lorenzo goes forth, murders him*
> *within, enters again.*

Lor. You must be sure to keep it secret now.
Perchance the king, to try your honesty,
And blind his daughter's eyes, will send to ask
Of's welfare.

Keep. O my lord!

Lor. Nay, I know you understand.   Farewell.

> [*Turns back again.*

One thing I had forgot : if any ask
What groan that was, say 'tis an usual thing
Against [a] great man's death to hear a noise
At midnight.   So now, royal lecher, set you safe,
'Tis your death must secure my life ; I'll on !
Danger is but a bug-word ; my barque shall through,
Did mountains of black horrors me surround.
When fortunes hang in doubt,
Bravely to dare is bravely to get out.

ACTUS II. SCŒNA I.

Lorenzo, Parmenio *attending.*

All leave the chamber ; if any come,
I'm busy.   Parmenio, be nigher—nigher yet :
What dar'st thou do to make thy master king,
Thyself a favourite?

Par. 'Tis something blunt, my lord ;   [*Studies.*
Why, I dare do—that which I dare not speak.

Lor. By all my hopes, spoke like the man I want !
'Twould be lost time to use much circumstance
To thee : shall we this night despatch the king?

Par. This minute, were he my father ;
He's not the first, nor shall he be the last.

Lor. Soul of my soul ! My better angel sure

Foresaw my wants, and sent thee hither.
Parmenio, there's none but he
Stands 'twixt a crown and me :
The cloud that interpos'd betwixt my hopes before
Is, like a vapour, fall'n, and seen no more.
The house of Clarimont is lost :
The king has sent one son to banishment,
And I have sent the father.
    Par. How, sir, you have not murdered him ?
                                [*Starts.*

    Lor. Why ?
    Par. Nothing, my lord ; only I'm sorry
I had no hand in't.
'Sdeath, hath the villain killed him ?   [*Aside.*
    Lor. O, thou art jealous !
Thy hand comes well enough ; this night
I have determined that soon, ere
The royal blood's a-tilt, you shall to horse.
'Tis easy to outride———
    Par. Imagination itself, my lord !
    Lor. For then report will say thou kill'dst him.
No matter.
    Par. O, none at all, my lord.
    Lor. When I am king, I can restore at ease.
    Par. True, my lord.   What, if
Your excellence cast out, when I am gone,
That Clarimont's youngest son did this, and took
His flight upon't.   His discontent's known well
      enough
To make of a suspicion a most received truth ;
Besides, wheresoever I go, I'll swear 'twas he.
    Lor. By Jove, most rare ; when I am king, I shall
Be poorer than I am, by giving thee
Thy due.   Away, let's lose no time in words,
We're both resolv'd to put this cause to swords.
I'll to the king : thou to prepare for night.
Four hours hence wait me in the gallery. [*Exeunt.*

ACTUS II.   SCŒNA II.

Enter CLARIMONT *solus.*

Break, heart, and burst !   My father murdered,
And in the midst of all his hopes of life !
Methinks I see millions of furies stand,
Ready to catch my rage's sacrifice,
O, for a man that could invent more plagues
Than hell could hold !   I have conceiv'd
Of wrong, and am grown great already.
O sweet revenge ! I humbly thee entreat
Be my grief's midwife ; let the mother die,
So thou bringst forth her long'd-for progeny.
Methinks I feel the villain grow within me,
And spread through all my veins.
How I could murder now, poison or stab !
My head is full of mischief.   Sulphur and flaming
    pitch
Shall be but mercy to those deaths I'll give.   [*Exit.*

ACTUS II.   SCŒNA III.

Enter the KING, *with* FIDELIO.

Fid. [Al]though it be not safe for subjects
To pry into the secrets of their prince,
Much less to question about them,
Yet the implicit faith of blind obedience,
Poison'd with pleasing oft—and 't like
Your majesty, why do you court this lady thus?
  King. Why dost thou ask?
  Fid. I know 'tis insolence to make reply,

Yet hear me as the echo of the court, great sir ;
They call your last-giv'n mercy and those favours
But fairer ends to lust.
   King. Thy zeal hath got thy pardon.
                                   [Stares upon him.
No more ; he that does offer to give direction
To his prince,'is full of pride, not of discretion. *[Exit.*
   Fid. So, to give kings good advice,
May show (I see) men faithful, but not wise :
I'm honest yet, and I do fare the worse for't
O' the court !
There humours reign, and merits only serve
To mock with idle hopes those best deserve.   *[Exit.*

ACTUS II. SCŒNA IV.

Enter FRANCELIA, BELLAMINO.

   Fran. Sir, leave your compliment ;
Methinks the sweetest speech is that that's meant.
   Bel. Wrong not my love, best creature, so to think
My words are not the true ambassadors
Of my heart ; by thy fair self, I swear,
Nature has been too partial in
Robbing heaven and earth to give you all——
   Fran. Their weaknesses you mean, and I confess,
     my lord——
   Bel. Their richest graces, sweetest ;
O, do not rack me thus !
I love : can you give love again ?
   Fran. Yes, any love that you dare ask,
Or I dare give, my lord.
   Bel. O, but, fair lady, love must have no bounds ;
It pines in prison.
   Fran. O, but, my lord, hot loves, if not contained,

Like fiery meteors, promise no good to others,
And are themselves consum'd.

      Enter the KING, *and* Lords *in attendance.*

    Bel. O, leave me not in doubt's distracting trance.
    King. How, my boy? what, courting?
    Bel. No, sir.
    King. What was he doing then, Francelia?
    Fran. So please your grace, he was i' th' midst
Of all your praises, when your highness enter'd.
    Bel. Hum! there's yet some hope then.   [*Aside.*
    King. O, you are glad we are come, then!
That discourse was tedious.
    Fran. No, my lord, I should have been well pleased
To have heard him longer.
    King. You are grown a courtier, fair one!
Sileo, are the coaches ready?
    Sil. Yes, and 't please your majesty.
    King. Come, we'll abroad then,
This day invites us forth; where's our queen?
                             [*Exeunt.*

ACTUS II. SCŒNA V.

Enter CLARIMONT, FIDELIO, *and young* FLORELIO.

    Clar. Then, with a pause fill'd up with sighs,
Ask him how strong his guards are; but, above all,
Be sure t' apply inflaming corrosives:
Screw up his anger to the height,
And make his fears be double.
Officious friends and mediation
May else prove remedies.
    Fid. Enough. If we do fail to act
Our parts to th' life in's tragedy,
May all those horrors that do threaten him
Fall upon us. Farewell.   [*Exeunt.*

Clar. So, my revenge flies high :
The villain first shall kill his father,
And while his hands are hot i' th' blood,
This sword shall pierce him.
Murdered he shall sink quick to hell,
I will not give him leave t' unload himself
Of one poor single sin of thought ;
But, lest he should wake out of 's great
Security, and shun his fate,
I will rock him on.
Mischiefs are like the cockatrice's eye :
If they see first, they kill ; if seen, they die.   [*Exit.*

ACTUS III.   SCŒNA I.

Enter KING, *young* FLORELIO, *and* FIDELIO.

King. And must the villain kill me too?
Flo. This very night.
King. Why, 'tis not possible ; what would he have
    had more ?
He had my heart, and might have had all but
The name of king !   O, heaven had tied
So strict a friendship, we could not part with 't ;
I durst have thought that I had merited
Fidelity from him.
Fid. O my lord, let ne'er so many drops,
Sweet as the morning dew, fall on the sea,
The brinish water turns them all to salt.
Where there's an ocean of ingratitude,
Favours must needs be lost.
King. Thou speak'st but truth
Who does to merit trust,
But writes an obligation in the dust.
Your counsels now my faithful life preserve,
Is there a way for pardon ?

Fid. Faith, sir, it
Would pollute mercy to use it here;
The fact's so foul,
It calls itself for death.
    King. And it shall have it.
Traitor's enough; but when ungrateful comes,
It stops the mouth of pity.   Go, take our guards,
And apprehend him straight.
    Flo. Soft, great sir,
'Twere fit your justice should consider
What way is made : if you shall apprehend him
For treason unborn, and which he only did intend,
Foolish report, which never was i' th' right,
May clear his guiltiness, and censure majesty.
If you'd permit him to approach the chamber,
(Yet who'd advise treason should come so near?)
You would take him in the act,
And leave no place for foul suspicion.
Then, if your grace sent for his father,
And kept him with pretence of business by you,
Till he became the witness of th' attempt,
Envy itself could have no cause to bark.
    King. Thou art my oracle; I cannot tell,
Whether my debt be greater to thy faith
Or to thy counsel.   Go and watch abroad;
And let these cares wait upon fate and me.
The captain of the guard 'twere fit you sounded;
He may do mischief.   Florelio, you
Shall to his father; the rest is mine to manage.
                                        [*Exeunt.*
These men are honest, and must be rewarded,
They do deserve it.   'Tis most rare to find
A greatness that enjoys true friends;
For commonly it makes us fear'd and hated.
The one doth breed offence : th' other leaves naked.
Let the impartial eye but look upon
All we call ours, and then again behold

The many hungry eyes of expectation
That wait upon our bounty, and it shall find
That we have scarce enough to keep men's hopes up,
We are rich if we can purchase friends.
Thrones, though they advance their glory ne'er so
    high,
Are but the seats of fear and misery.   [*Exit.*

ACTUS III.   SCŒNA II.

Enter PARMENIO *and* LORENZO.

Par. In deep security, my lord,
The lady's at one window courted;
The king, with Florelio and the favourite,
Contriving of a masque, which he
Must never see.
    Lor. Good! which he must never see.
O, thou dost hug my fates!
How I am ravished to think upon
Ensuing joys!   Parmenio,
He's dead already.
    Par. Six hours ago, my lord, you cannot think
How much ado I had to keep myself
From saying, "And 't shall please your majesty,"
I' th' open presence to you.   Methinks
One while I see your highness sit like Jupiter
In state, with all the petty gods about you;
And then again, in a more tempting shape
Than was the shower of gold,
Lie in some Danae's lap;
More wanton than Europa's bull!
Another time, with some great train,
As if you went to battle,
Rock'd in a downy coach, go take the air,
And have the thronging city

Crowded into a handful, looking
Along to bless your eyes, and striving
Who shall cry loudest, " God bless your majesty ! "
   Lor. And all the while thou, like my Ganymede,
Shalt taste ambrosia with me, while the petty gods
Burst with repining at thy happiness.
Thou shalt dispose of all, create, displace,
Be call'd my boy, revel and masque, what not?
O, for one half-year
I will not speak unto the people,
Take you that office, keep that part for yours.
O, how I long for night !
Thou can'st not name the pleasure,
Could make the time not tedious.
Away unto thy watch ; and when the king's a-bed,
Be here.
   Par. I shall, my lord—
And 't please your majesty, I shall.   [*Exeunt.*

ACTUS III. SCŒNA III.

Enter the QUEEN AMASIA, BELLAMINO *her favourite,*
DROLLIO, *Attendants.*

   Bel. What is the matter, madam, that the court
Is in such clouds to-night ?   The king
Feigns mirth and freeness, but withal
Flashes of fury make escapes.
   Queen. 'Tis strange, my lord, you should not know.
   Bel. Faith, madam, I know nothing.
   Queen. Troth, nor I ; but I suspect.
The clock no sooner struck, but all the statesmen
Started, as if they had been to run a race,
And the king told me 'twere fit I took my rest.
There's something in't ; but these designs of state
We women know no more than our own fate.

To turn our talk—faith, my lord, where lies
That beauty, that so captivates you all?
She has a graceful garb, 'tis true.

Bel. Who, madam? Francelia? O, she has
A dainty foot and daintier hand;
An eye, round as a globe, and black as jet:
So full of majesty and life, that when
It most denies, it most invites.

Queen. These parts she has indeed; but is here all?
Bel. All? heaven forbid!
Her hair is so preciously fair and soft,
That were she fall'n into some river, and
In danger, one would make a conscience
To save her life, for fear of spoiling it.
Her lips are gently swelled, like unto
Some blushing cherry, that hath newly tasted
The dew from heaven; and her cheeks——

Queen. Hold, hold, my lord; all this is poetry!
A painter could not flatter more.
To my eye now, she is so slender,
She's scarce, I think, a span about i' th' middle.

Bel. O madam! you must think wise Nature,
Of such rich mould as she was framed,
Would make as little waste as could be!

Queen. So, so.
What think you of the upper part o' th' nose, then;
Does it not look as if, did it [1] give way,
The eyes should shortly have an interview?

Bel. You're too severe a critic, madam;
So good a wit as yours should make,
Where there were any,[2] all bless'd perfections.
After all, next to your highness, I'm resolved
To think she is chiefest beauty.

---

[1] [Old copy, *it did.*]
[2] [So old copy; perhaps we ought to read, *Were there not any.*]

Queen. Not next to me, my lord ; now I am sure
    you flatter,
But 'tis too late to chide you for it.
Good night.   [*Exeunt.*

ACTUS III. SCŒNA IV.

Enter the KING *going to bed,* CLEONAX, *Lords,*
Attendants.

King. Good night to all. Lord Cleonax, a word in
    private ;   [*Whisper.*
Take away the lights, and shut the door.   [*Exeunt.*

Enter PARMENIO *and* LORENZO.

Lor. Is the king gone to bed?
Par. An hour ago, my lord.
Lor. What if he should not be asleep yet?
Par. No matter ; ere his tongue can speak, our
    swords
Shall kill. What, though he call us traitors?
'Twill be his last, and may be pardoned. Come,
Sir, bravely on ! fear's worse than death,
You're lord of all, or not of your own breath.
    Lor. Nay, if I fear, may I not live ! Follow.
         [*The King calls out, Treason ! Old Cleonax,*
               rising to go out at the door to call for help,
               is met by his son, who took him for the
               King, and killed him : Lorenzo is presently
               of set purpose run through by Parmenio.

ACTUS III. SCŒNA V.

Enter the KING *in his nightgown, Lords, Attendants.*

    King. Trust me, most sad and strange !
A flood of grief beats at my eyes for vent.
Poor Cleonax, I'm truly sorry for thee.

Lords. So are we all.

King. This accident
Commands our pity; but what is done, is done.
Let it not be as yet divulged.   Remove
The corpse, and let it be the care of thee,
Florelio, to see his burial honourable
And private.   Good thanks to all the rest.
Clarimont, stay you with me.   [*Exeunt.*
The traitor's dead, [and] by Parmenio; but
You must know there's one yet lives within me—
I love, Clarimont.

Clar. That passion of all others,
Sir, heaven easiliest pardons :
He lives not, sure, that love's not.

King. Ay, but my love's not pure.   'Tis great,
Not good, Clarimont.   I love Francelia !

Clar. Take heed of unchaste fires, great sir :
They mischief, sir.   Forget her, faith, forget her.
Such fits as these are ever cur'd like agues—
Best when they are most starved.
If you shall give them their desired fuel,
They'll not be quench'd with ease, and it
Is ever seen (heaven keep my sovereign !)
The house they're bred in feels them first and ever.

King. Clarimont, thou wert ne'er in love;
Thou art philosophical, and wouldst have reason
Guide where it was never yet companion.
Thou show'st thy want of love,
But helpst not mine.   Counsel is now too late;
It's like smith's water flung upon the coals
Which more inflames.   Here.
Thou twice hast sav'd my life, if thou now speed'st;
Go to Francelia, and present
This jewel to her, and withal my love.
                              [*Gives him a jewel.*
Do't with thy best of language and respect.
Fair means at first we'll use,

But foul shall come, if she the fair refuse.
Good night, and good success.
    Clar. Obedience is the best of what I am,
Your will's my law, sir.   [*Exit.*
Why, then, it must be.
Was there no woman in the court
To feed thy lust with, but my sister ;
And none to be the bawd, but I ?
Couldst thou not think of any other way
T' express thy greatness, but by doing me wrong ?
My father's angry ghost, I see, is not
Full appeased yet.   Why should I make   [*Studies.*
Of murther thus begun a massacre ?
He did my father right in his revenge ;
Ay, but he wrong'd him first ; and yet, who knows
But it was justice to attempt by force ?
The removal of great favourites, though enemies
To th' state, is not so warrantable—
I'm in a maze.
Something I'll do, but what I cannot tell,
I fear the worst ; lust never ended well.   [*Exit.*

ACTUS IV. SCŒNA I.

Enter FRANCELIA *and* BELLAMINO.

    Fran. Fie, leave this importunity, my lord,
I shall yield else, by this kiss I shall.
    Bel. By this, and this, and this, thou shalt !
Heavens, what a breath is here !
Thy father fed on musk and amber,
When he begot thee, sure ? The wanton air,
Chaf'd by the hot scents of Arabic spices,
Is nothing nigh so sweet ; the ambrosia,
The gods themselves were drunk with,
Dwells on thy lips.

Enter FLORELIO, *senior, but stands aside.*

Fran. Come, come, you flatter,
'Tis on yours, my lord.
 Bel. On mine?   Alas,
Nature gave us the prickles, you the roses,
But meant that they should grow together.
            [*Kisses again.*
 Fran. So, so; what, if the King or Florelio saw ye?
 Bel. What, if they did?   I can fear nothing now
But surfeits.   Come, we lose time, my fairest,
Do we not? this is the minute.   [*Kisses her again.*
 Flo. By heaven, this is not fair, madam.
 Fran. Wonder strikes me dumb.   [*Exit.*
 Flo. How does she kiss, favourite?
 Bel. Who, my lord?
 Flo. My wife, my lord.   Draw, draw, or by all my
   hopes,
My rage will make me turn a murderer.
 Bel. Not so easily.   [*They fight.*
 Flo. Hold, let's breathe: why should I do him
   right,
Who has done me such wrong, or die for her
That will not live for me?   [*Puts up.*
Go, enjoy her!   [*Offers to go out.*
 Bel. Soft, you have stol'n a secret here,
            [*Pulls him back.*
That you must give again, or take my life.
Draw.
 Flo. Pr'ythee, disturb me not.
 Bel. No, unless you promise never to disclose,
What you have here discovered,
This must be the passage.
       [*Stands betwixt the door and him.*
 Flo. Hum ! I will be mute, credit me,
I will not speak one word.   [*Offers to go out again.*
 Bel. Nay, you must swear it too. [*Pulls him back.*

Flor. If I must, I must.
By heaven and by my honour,
How tame a thing a cuckold is !   [*Exit.*
  Bel. 'Sdeath, why did I let him go?
We can no more subsist together
Than fire and water.   One of us two must die ;
And charity tells me, better he than I.
But how? it is not for my honour
To kill him basely ; nor is it   [*Studies.*
For hers to kill him otherwise ;
Th' whole court will guess the quarrel,
If it be a duel.   [*Studies again.*
It is decreed ; no matter which way, so he fall :
Mine, in respect of hers, are no respects at all. [*Exit.*

ACTUS IV.   SCŒNA II.

Enter DOCODISAPIO *and* DROLLIO.

  Doc. Abused, grossly abused ! a base affront,
Believe it, Drollio.
  Drol. Why, what's the matter, signior?
  Doc. Why, do you hear nothing?
  Drol. No.   Why, what should it be?
  Doc. Pisaro is the man.
  Drol. Fie, fie ! it cannot be ;
The state could not commit so great an oversight,
Neglect a man of merit for Pisaro.   Fie, fie !
  Doc. Want of judgment, Drollio.
An unlearned council : I ever told you so ;
Never more heads, nor never less wit, believe't.
  Drol. Say you so, signior? that's hard.
What say you to Diano?
  Doc. Alas ! an ordinary brain ;
Talks and talks, it's true,
But speaks more than he is, believe't.

Betwixt you and I, a mere prattler.
There's Falorio, too ; why, he cannot read his own
    hand ;
Vasquez cannot speak sense without two days'
Premeditation.   Sillio, Vechio, Caronnio—
All stones in their head !
    Drol. If I should tell these lords now, signior,
What you say, it might cost an ear or so.
    Doc. Ay.   Why, there's another abuse i' th' state :
A man shall have his ears cut off for speaking
A truth.[1]   A sick government, Drollio,
And a weak one, believe't.   It never thrived,
Since Spain and we grew so great.
There is a mystery in that too, Drollio.
I will know all before they have
Any more of my money——
    Drol. Peace, signior.   The king !   [*Exeunt.*

Enter the KING, QUEEN, *Lords, an* Ambassador *from
    Spain, who has his audience; after which the*
    KING *goes out talking with* FIDELIO, *the rest follow.
    Then enter the two brothers* FLORELIO ; *the elder
    speaks earnestly.*

    Flor. sen. I pr'ythee, leave me ; by all that's good,
Thou canst not know it.   Why shouldst thou thus
In vain torment thyself and me ?   [*They whisper.*
    Flor. jun. Well, I guess, and 'tis enough.
                  [*Exeunt at several doors.*

---

[1] [An allusion, perhaps, to the fate of Prynne.]

ACTUS IV. SCŒNA III.

Enter CLARIMONT *and* FRANCELIA.

Fran. Think not, good sir, your elegant enforce-
 ments
Can seduce my weak [1] innocence ; it's a
Resolution grounded ; and
Sooner shall the
Fixed orbs be lifted off their hinges,
Than I be mov'd to any act that bears
The name of foul. You know the way you came,
 sir ?
 Clar. Is this all the respect the king shall have ?
No, you would do well to clothe this harsh denial
In better language.
 Fran. You may please to say,
I owe my life unto my sovereign,
And should be proud to pay it in
At any warning, were it ne'er so short.
But for my chastity, it doth so much concern another
I can by no means part with it :
So fare you well, sir.   [*Exit.*
 Clar. By heaven, a saint, no woman !
Sure, she was born o' th' virtues of her mother,
Not of her vices.[2] The whole sex
May come to be thought well of for her sake.
I long to meet Florelio ; my joy is not complete,
Till I have cured his jealousies as well as mine.
                                                 [*Exit.*

Enter FLORELIO *and a* Boy.

 Flor. There was a time,
When snakes and adders had no being :

---

[1] [Old copy, *weaker.*]   [2] [Old copy, *Nieces.*]

When the poor infant-world had no worse reptiles,
Than were the melon and the strawberry !
Those were the golden times of innocence.
There were no kings then, nor no lustful peers,
No smooth-fac'd favourites, nor no cuckolds, sure.
O, how happy is that man, whose humbler thoughts
Kept him from court ; who never yet was taught   X
The glorious way unto damnation !
Who never did aspire
Further than the cool shades of quiet rest.
How have the heavens his lower wishes bless'd.
Sleep makes his labours sweet, and innocence
Does his mean fortunes truly recompense :
He feels no hot loves, nor no palsy-fears,
No fits of filthy lusts, or of pale jealousies :
He wants, it's true, our clothes, our masks, our
    diet,
And wants our cares, our fears, and our disquiets.
But this is all but raving,
And does distemper more.   I'll sleep :
                    [*Lies all along on the ground.*
Boy, sing the song I gave you.

A Song to a Lute.

Hast thou seen the dawn i' th' air,
        when wanton blasts have toss'd it;
Or the ship on the sea,
        when ruder waves have cross'd it ?
Hast thou mark'd the crocodile's weeping,
        or the fox's sleeping ?
Or hast view'd the peacock in his pride,
        or the dove by his bride,
        when he courts for his lechery ?
O, so fickle, O, so vain, O, so false, so false is she !

Flor. Good boy, leave me !   [*Boy exit.*

Enter CLARIMONT.

Clar. How now, Florelio, melancholy?

Flor. No, I was studying. Pr'ythee, resolve me,
Whether it be better to maintain
A strong, implicit faith, that can
By no means be oppress'd ;
Or, falling to the bottom at the first,
Arm'd with disdain and with contempt, to scorn the
worst ?

    Clar. This is a subtle one ; but why studying about
    this ?

    Flor. Faith, I would find a good receipt for the
    headache,
That's all.

    Clar. Hum, I know now whereabouts you are ;
No more on't. I'm come to clear those doubts—
Your wife is chaste, chaste as the turtledove.

    Flor. Ha, ha, ha !

    Clar. Ha? why do you laugh? I know she is ;
    'tis not
So many hours, since I tempted her
With all my eloquence, and for the king,
Yet found her cold as ice.

    Flor. Ha, ha, ha !

    Clar. You do not well to tempt a friend ;
You do forget she is my sister.

    Flor. I would I ne'er had known you had one.

    Clar. You'll give a reason now for this.

    Flor. None.

    Clar. By all that's good, since our dear father left
    us,
We are become his scorn ; look you, sir,
I dare maintain it.   [*Draws.*

    Flor. But I dare not. Put up, put up, young man,
When thou hast known a woman,
Thou wilt be tamer.   [*Exit.*

Clar. Ha! what should this mean?
I know he's valiant, wise, discreet;
And what of that? Passion, when it hath got the bit,
Doth ofttimes throw the rider.
Yet why should I be peremptory?
She may, for aught I know, be yet unchaste
With some unworthy groom.[1]   *[Studies.*
What if I stole into some corner,
And heard her at confession? 'Twould not be amiss;
For souls at such a time, like ships in tempests,
Throw out all they have; and now I think on't,
Her trial shall be quick.   Friend, I'll do thee right,
Come on't what will, she dies, if she be light.   *[Exit.*

ACTUS IV.   SCŒNA IV.

Enter SIGNIOR MULTECARNI *the Poet, and*
two of the Actors.

Mul. Well, if there be no remedy, one must act
        two parts;
Rosselio shall be the fool and the lord,
And Tisso the citizen and the cuckold.
    1 *Act.* That cannot be, signior, you know,
One still comes in, when the other goes out.
    Mul. By Jove, 'tis true.   Let me see,
We'll contrive it : the lord and the usurer,
The citizen and the politician;
And sure they never are together.
But who shall act the honest lawyer? [2]
'Tis a hard part, that!

---

[1] [*i.e.,* Fellow or man.   The word is often used by our old
writers in this sense.]
[2] [Suckling, perhaps, had in his recollection a play with this
title by S. S., printed in 1616.]

2 *Act.* And a tedious one,
It's admired [1] you would put it in, squire;
And 'tis against your own rules
To represent anything on the stage
That cannot be.
    Mul. Why, dost think
'Tis impossible for a lawyer to be honest?
    1 *Act.* As 'tis for a lord treasurer to be poor,
Or for a king not to be cosened.
There's little Robin, in debt within these three years,
Grown fat and full by the trade:
And then there's Borachio, an unknown man,
Got it all by speaking loud and bawling:
Believe it, signior, they have no more conscience
Than an innkeeper.
    Mul. I grant you all this;
An old cook and a good will please all palates.
There's that for the young tapers of the law;
Then there's a bawdy jest or two
Extraordinary for the ladies;
And, when it comes to be acted in private,
I'll have a jerk at the state for the country gentlemen.
If it does not take, my masters,
It lies not upon me; I've provided well.
And if the stomach of the times be naught,
The fault's not in the meat or in the cook.
Come, let us find out Lepido,
And dine at the Mermaid.
Come, let us have one rouse,[2] my Joves, in Aristippus,
We shall conceive the better afterwards.
    Act. Agreed, agreed.   [*Exeunt singing.*

    Come, come away, to the tavern, I say,
    For now at home is washing-day:
    Leave your prittle-prattle, let's have a pottle,
    We are not so wise as Aristotle.

---

    [1] [Wondered.]   [2] [A *rouse* is a bumper.]

ACTUS IV. SCŒNA V.

Enter CLARIMONT *and* FLORELIO.

Clar. By heaven she's false, false as the tears of
    crocodiles,
Or what is yet more feign'd, I do confess.
Your pardon, Florelio, come, pray your pardon ;
Perchance I may deserve it.
    Flor. You have it, so has she ;
Would heaven would do it as easily as I.
    Clar. Heaven cannot do so foul an act.
She has,—O, she has done too much !
And should not I see justice done,
The gods would punish me. Brother, clear up,
The world shall not be one day elder, ere
I see thy injuries revenged. This night
The king will revel, and be gamesome :
He will change beds with thee.
Deny him not, and leave the rest to me.
    Flor. Thy youth, I see, doth put thee on too fast,
Thou hast too much of passion, gentle brother.
Thinkst thou the death of a poor lustful king
Or peer can give me ease. No ;
For, if it could, my hand durst go as far
That way as thine.
Had she been chaste, there had no tempters been,
Or if there had, I had not thought it sin.
Draw not thy sword at all, I do beseech thee,
'Twill not deserve one drop of noble blood ;
Forget it, do, for my sake.
    Clar. May heaven forget me then !
Where is the courage of thy house become ?
When didst thou cease to be thyself? Shall two
Brave families be wrong'd—most basely wrong'd—

And shall we tamely, like philosophers,
Dispute it with [1] our reasons?
First may I live the scorn of all the world,
Then die forgotten! No, no;
Were there as many actors in thy wrong,
As does the vast stage of the world now bear,
Not one should 'scape my rage: I and my ghost
Would persecute them all.
By all our ties, of love, of brother, friend:
By what thou holdst most dear, I do conjure thee
To leave this work to me; and if
E'er thou canst think that I present thee not
A full revenge, then take it out on me.

    Flor. Thy zeal hath overcome me;
What wouldst thou have me do?

    Clar. Nothing but this:
Obey the king in all he shall desire,
And let your servants be at my dispose
This night. One of your faithful'st confidants
Send hither presently.

    Flor. Well, I shall; but what you'll do,
Heav'n knows: I know not, nor will I.
It is enough that I (against my will)
Am made a passive instrument of ill.
Farewell.   [*Exit.*

    Clar. So there is but this:
The wanton king this night thinks to embrace
My sister; his bed shall prove his grave.
His own favourite shall make it so;
I have persuaded him she yields,
And this night does expect him:
He, to make sure o' th' husband,
By my advice, as if he did intend
Some jest, means to change lodgings
With wrong'd Florelio the favourite.

---

[1] [Old copy, *without.*]

Enter PETRUCHIO.

O Petruchio, welcome! You have other clothes;
These I would [1] borrow for a little while:
In masquing times disguises are in fashion.
I have a pretty plot in hand; and if it take,
'Twill be some crowns in thy way.
　　Pet. I shall pray hard it may, sir;
My clothes, howsoever, are at your service.
　　Clar. And I at yours, Petruchio.
But you must be dumb and secret now.
　　Pet: As any statue, sir.
　　Clar.　　　　　　Come, then, let us about it.
　　　　　　　　　　　　　　　　　[Exeunt.

ACTUS V.　SCŒNA I.

Enter LEPIDO *and* DROLLIO.

　　Drol. A rare masque, no doubt; who contriv'd it?
　　Lep. Marry, he that says 'tis good, howsoe'er he
　　　　has made it,
Signior Multecarni.
　　Drol. Who, the poet-laureate?
　　Lep. The same.
　　Drol. O, then, 'twere blasphemy to speak against it.
What, are we full of Cupids?
Do we sail upon the vast, and re-sail,
And fetch the masque from the clouds?
　　Lep. Away, critic, thou never understoodst him.
　　Drol. Troth, I confess it; but my comfort is,
Others are troubled with the same disease,
'Tis epidemical, Lepido; take't on my word,
And so let's in, and see how things go forward.
　　　　　　　　　　　　　　　　　[Exeunt.

---

　　　[1] [Old copy, *should.*]

ACTUS V. SCŒNA II.

Enter FRANCELIA *alone, weeping.*

Swell on, my griefs, and O, ye gentler tears,
Drop still, and never cease to fall,
Till you become a boundless ocean !
Then drown the source that sent you out, and hide
Francelia from her husband's sight,
Her wronged husband's.   O,
Could my Florelio but see,
How all hot flames within me are gone forth,
Sure, he would love again.   Yet sure
He would not.   Heavens ! how just you are,
And, O, how wicked am I ! ![1]
My heart beats thick, as if my end were nigh ;
And would it were ! a better time death
Cannot take ; an absolution I have had,
And have confess'd my unchaste love
Unto my ghostly father.   My peace is made above,
But here below?—What mak'st thou here,
Petruchio?

Enter CLARIMONT *like to Petruchio.*

Clar. She weeps ; the whore repents perchance.
[Aside.

Madam,
It is my master's pleasure that this night
You keep your chamber.
   Fran. Thy voice and countenance are not the
        same ;
They tell me that thy master is displeased.
   Clar. Madam, it may be so ; but that to me

---

[1] [Old copy, *I am.*]

Is as unknown as is the new-found world.
I am his servant, and obey commands.
   Fran. And so am I.   I pr'ythee tell him so ;
I will not stir.   [*Exit.*
   Clar. How cunning is
The devil in a woman's shape !   He had
Almost again persuaded me
To have become her brother.

Enter Servant.

   Ser. Petruchio, the favourite is lighted at the door,
And asks to see my lady.
   Clar. My lady is retired ; where is he ?
                    [*Exit Servant.*
This to my heart's desire falls out.

Enter BELLAMINO *the favourite.*

   Bel. Where is Francelia ?
   Clar.   My lord, she is not well,
And craves your lordship's pardon.
   Bel. What, sick upon a masque-night,
And when the king sends for her !
Come, come, that must not be ;
Which way is she ?
     [*Clarimont steps to him and whispers.   He starts.*
   Bel. By heaven !
   Clar. By heaven, nor will she ever see you more,
If he——
   Bel. I understand you.   I am Bellamino.
If e'er he see the morning.   I had decreed it ;
Nor should he have surviv'd three days,
Had he been ne'er so silent.   This night's
His last, Petruchio.   This arm shall make it so.
I will not trust my brother with the act.
   Clar. Nobly resolv'd ; but how or where, my
     lord ?

Bel. No matter where.   Rather than fail,
I'll make the presence chamber be
The place of execution.
    Clar.   Still nobly ;
But, my lord——
    Bel.   .   But again, Petruchio?
    Clar. And again, my lord.
Why, think you that Petruchio, when he is
Entrusted in a business, will not see
It rightly done, and for his lady's honour?
You'll kill him, and in public ; then, forsooth,
When you're i' th' saddle, all the court shall cry,
Francelia was weary of her husband.
No, no ; my lady loves you well,
But loves her honour too ; and there are ways (I hope)
To keep the one, and yet not lose the other.
Do not I know my lady lies alone,
And will feign herself sick this night,
And all on purpose too ? am not I to let you
Into her chamber,
And to give out, the fact once done,
That he killed himself.——[1]

---

[1] [The play ends here imperfectly.]

LETTERS.

Letters to divers Eminent Personages : written on several occa-
sions. By Sir John Svckling. Printed by his own copy.

Printed imperfectly in 1646 and 1648, but with considerable
additions in 1658, according to the bookseller's statement, from
originals supplied to him by the poet's sister, Lady Southcot, to
whom the third edition is inscribed in terms which countenance
such a fact.

Very few of these interesting, witty, and sensible epistles bear
any indication of the persons to whom they were addressed; but
several are directed to one and the same lady, perhaps her from
whom he took some hints for " Aglaura."

Letters.

———o———

[*To William Davenant.*[1]]

WILL,—It is reported here a-shipboard that the
wind is, as women are, for the most part bad : that it
altogether takes part with the water, for it crosses him
continually that crosses the seas : that it is not good
for a state-reserved politician to come to sea, for he is
subject to lay forth his mind in very plain terms : that
it is an ill gaming[2] place, for four days together here
has been very bad casting of all sides, and I think if
we had tarried longer it would have been worse : that
so much rope is a needless thing in a ship, for they
drown here altogether, not hang : that if a wench at
land or a ship at sea spring a leak, 'tis fit and necessary they should be pump'd : that Dunkirk is the
Papist's purgatory, for men are fain to pay money to
be freed of it ; or, to speak more like a true Protestant, it is the water-hell, for if a man 'scape this, 'tis

---

[1] Ashm. MS. 826, fol. 101.   Now first printed.
[2] MS. *gaminng.*

ten to one he shall be saved : that lying four nights a-shipboard is almost as bad as sitting up to lose money at threepenny gleek, and so pray tell Mr Brett ; and thus much for sea-news.

Since my coming ashore, I find that the people of this country are a kind of infidels, not believing in the Scripture ; for though it be there promised there shall never be another Deluge, yet they do fear it daily, and fortify against it : that they are Nature's youngest children, and so, consequently, have the least portion of wit and manners ; or rather that they are her bastards, and so inherit none at all. And sure their ancestors, when they begot them, thought on nothing but monkeys and boars and asses, and such like ill-favoured creatures ; for their physiognomies are so wide from the rules of proportion, that I should spoil my prose to let in the description of them. In a word, they are almost as bad as those of Leicestershire ; their habits are as monstrous as themselves to all strangers. But by my troth, to speak the naked truth of them, the difference betwixt the dressing of their women and ours is only this—these bombast their tails, and ours their arms. As for the country, the water and the King of France beleaguer it round. Sometimes the Hollander gets ground upon them ; sometimes they upon him. It is so even a level that a man must have more than the quantity of a grain of mustard-seed in faith to remove a mountain here, for there is none in the country. Their own turf is their firing altogether, and it is to be feared that they will burn up their country before doomsday. The air, what with their breathing in it and its own natural corruption, is so unwholesome that a man must resolve to be at the charge of an ague once a month. The plague is here constantly—I mean excise—and in so great a manner that the whole country is sick on't. Our very farts stand us in I know not how much excise to the states before we let them. To be learned here is capital treason of them, believing that *fortuna favet fatuis*; and therefore, that they may have the better success in their wars, they choose burgomasters and burghers, as we do our mayors and aldermen, by their great bellies, little wits, and full purses. Religion they use as a stuff cloak in summer, more for show than anything else, their *summum bonum* being altogether wealth. They wholly busy themselves about it; not a man here but would do that which Judas did for half the money. To be short, the country is stark nought, and yet too good for the inhabitants; but being our allies, I will forbear their character and rest.—Your humble servant,

J. SUCKLING.

LONDON,[1] *Nov. 18th*, 1629.

[*To Sir Henry Vane.*][2]

RIGHT HONOURABLE,—What my journey through France afforded, your lordship had in haste from Dover by the way of Antwerp. On Tuesday I arrived at Court, and came soon enough to find the face of it extremely changed. Looking asquint upon you in Germany, as well as upon all of us that were sent from thence, the fault at first I laid upon the night and my own bad eyes; but the next day made it clear and plain. The packet to my Lord Treasurer I presented

---

[1] [Although dated from London, it seems doubtful whether this letter was really written there; it rather seems to have been penned and despatched somewhere on Suckling's route homeward from Dunkirk.]

[2] ["Domestic Papers, Charles I.," No. 216, p. 6. Now first printed. See "Calendars," 1631-3, p. 322. The facsimile of Suckling's handwriting is taken from this letter.]

first, and the taking of Donawart, who both to the bearer and the news showed alike indifferent, something cool if not cold, perchance his garb. From thence I went to the king, and made my way by Maxfield, Murray being not there. His majesty was well content the king was still victorious, but took it not so hot as those of France, nor did he at first conceive of it of so great importance. The bedchamber-men were most of them there, and the king spoke loud. That little, therefore, I had to say to him from Sir Isaac Wake and your lordship I reserved for a more private audience, that I might see something more into the king's mind. Master Murray would have had it been the next morning; but I deferred it a day, and having seen my Lord of Middlesex, and spoken with your son, I found, as I conceived, the reason of what I so much wondered at, and a better way than otherwise perchance I had taken. Before, therefore, I went to the king, I attended my Lord Treasurer, and told him that by more particular command I was more specially to wait upon his lordship; that I was to speak to the king that morning, but was come before to kiss his lordship's hands. And having in a manner repeated what I was to say, because I knew that which I had both from you and Sir Isaac Wake was something too much Sweden and monarchy, I mingled with it the noise of the Spaniards' passing the Moselle, the confirmation of the Landgrave of Hessen's defeat, and the voted forces of Wallenstein (of which I conceived by circumstance you write nothing), all which more specially he commanded me to represent to his majesty. In the conclusion I told him, that if there were anything in what I had said that could seem less fit to his lordship, or anything besides that his lordship could think more fit, I stood there ready to be disposed of by him, upon which he embraced me, thanked your lordship more

especially for that address, promised to send away
presently to you, and willed me to attend, while he
came to the king, that he might present me, which he
did. The king was very well pleased and satisfied :
much better than he was at my first appearing. He
questioned me much and about many things ; resolved
for a despatch, but seemed to refer it to my Lord
Treasurers. He conceived you had . . . . already,
but yet should have more since you required them.
Thus things have passed in show well in this last act.
By the despatch itself you will easily judge, whether
really be intended or no ; if, after all this delay, it be
full and without reserves, the fears of all those, that
honour you and . . . . you, are at an end. Howsoever, though there be some, yet the next from you
I receive will take them all away. The disposal of
the Cofferer's place after this manner makes the
world think that there is some staggering in the
friendship betwixt my Lord Treasurer and you, if not a
breach ; and those that are of Sir Thomas Roe's Cabinet
would persuade that you were sent over to undo the
affairs of the King of Swede and your own. Many
that really wish you well begin to imagine that you
shall be kept there 'longer than you would. If there
be any such thing, the causes certainly will be these :
first, your greatness with my Lord Marquis, and your
too strict intelligence one with another, which is here
represented to the full. And howsoever your lordship thinks things are reconciled betwixt my Lord
Treasurer and him, yet they say otherwise here, and
the effects speak no less. No man dares think well
of him here, and by what your son and . . . .
observed, it is easy to believe the king's ears himself
has been a little too open to the reports. I do him all
the service I can, where I find it may do any good,
though I know Jacob Ashley has lost himself about
the same thing. That which may, in a second place,

be considerable, will be your too lively representations, making the King of Swede to outrage the Emperor more than they will allow him here to do. And indeed your lordship's case in this is not much unlike that of Sharnes's; for where you are, they thought you too much a Spaniard, and here they think you all much a Spaniard. Then, again, the women take it ill that your son should be a statesman before theirs; and my Lady Weston has let fall in a manner so much to my Lord Vane. Besides, which I conceive [as of] more importance, larger instructions were by him carried to the king than to my Lord Treasurer, and sooner. Last of all, whether your lordship's clerks have in your absence followed your directions or no, or whether they have behaved themselves ill or well in the issuing out and disposing of moneys, I cannot tell; but, I suspect, a sinister report has been made of all. Your person would certainly be necessary here; and I make no doubt your wisdom will find out the quickest and best way for it, unless you yourself (as it well may be after all this) know, that all the world on this side of the seas are in errors. That which makes me any way stagger in my hopes of your sudden coming home is, that the King of Swede knows too well that, England satisfied in the demands of the Palatinate, and things at a full point concerning that particular, this crown will no longer make court to him, and after it he must expect no great matters from hence. Besides, France, which in show pretends to go along with us, really, perchance, intends nothing less, since there is nothing but that of the Palatinate that can keep Spain and us from tying a more strict knot together, and nothing but that that has kept us so long asunder. And the ill will be that, if his majesty of Swede make larger progress and be more fortunate, we shall here fear him as too great, or he himself will be more difficult. If he be less successful, we shall not conclude with him as too weak. And now, my lord, your lordship has what we talk here. I am not peremptory that things are so as I have here represented them ; but I am certain they are thought to be so. Your lordship's better judgment will resolve it, and I am more than confident will yet bring everything to its right place. You have many here that can do more towards it, but none that more sincerely wishes it than

Mar 2, 1682. Whitehall.

Y'r humble servant, Jo. Suckling.

If your lordship would please to think it fit to send at random—and by any messengers rather than none—the news, it would not certainly be amiss.

[*To Aglaura(?)*]

FORTUNE and love have ever been so incompatible, that it is no wonder, madam, if, having had so much of the one for you, I have ever found so little of the other for myself. Coming to the town, and having rid as if I had brought intelligence of a new-landed enemy to the State, I find you gone the day before, and with you, madam, all that is considerable upon the place ; for, though you have left behind you faces whose beauties might well excuse perjury in others, yet in me they cannot, since to the making that no sin love's casuists have most rationally resolved that she for whom we forsake ought to be handsomer than the forsaken, which would be here impossible. So that now a gallery, hung with Titian's or Vandyke's hand, and a chamber filled with living excellence, are the same things to me ; and the use that I shall make of that sex now will be no other than that which the wiser sort of Catholics do of pictures—at the highest, they but serve to raise my devotion to you. Should a great beauty now resolve to take me in (as that is all they think belongs to it) with the artillery of her eyes, it would be as vain as for a thief to set upon a new-robbed passenger. You, madam, have my heart already ; nor can you use it unkindly but with some injustice, since, besides that it left a good service to wait on you, it was never known to stay so long or so willingly before with any. After all, the wages will not be high, for it hath been brought up under Platonics, and knows no other way of being paid for service than by being commanded more ; which truth when you doubt, you have but to send to its master and your humble servant, J. S.

A Dissuasion from Love.

JACK,—Though your disease be in the number of those that are better cured with time than precept, yet, since it is lawful for every man to practise upon them that are forsaken and given over (which I take to be your state), I will adventure to prescribe to you ; and of the innocence of the physic you shall not need to doubt, since I can assure you I take it daily myself.

To begin methodically, I should enjoin you travel ; for absence doth in a kind remove the cause, removing the object, and answers the physician's first recipe, vomiting and purging ; but this would be too harsh, and indeed not agreeing to my way. I therefore advise you to see her as often as you can ; for, besides that the rarity of visits endears them, this

may bring you to surprise her, and to discover little
defects which, though they cure not absolutely, yet
they qualify the fury of the fever. As near as you
can, let it be unseasonably: when she is in sickness
and disorder, for that will let you know she is mortal,
and a woman; and the last would be enough to a wise
man. If you could draw her to discourse of things
she understands not, it would not be amiss.

Contrive yourself often into the company of the
cried-up beauties; for if you read but one book, it
will be no wonder if you speak or write that style:
variety will breed distraction, and that will be a kind
of diverting the humour.

I would not have you deny yourself the little things,
for these agues are easier cured with surfeits than
abstinence; rather, if you can, taste all, for that, as
an old author saith, will let you see—

> That the thing for which we woo
> Is not worth so much ado.

But since that here would be impossible, you must
be content to take it where you can get it. And this
for your comfort I must tell you, Jack, that mistress
and woman differ no otherwise than Frontiniac and
ordinary grapes; which, though a man loves never so
well, yet, if he surfeit of the last, he will care but little
for the first.

I would have you leave that foolish humour, Jack,
of saying you are not in love with her, and pretending
you care not for her; for smothered fires are dangerous, and malicious humours are best and safest
vented and breathed out. Continue your affection
to your rival still; that will secure you from one way
of loving, which is in spite, and preserve your friendship with her woman, for who knows but she may
help you to the remedy?

A jolly glass and right company would much conduce to the cure; for though in the Scripture (by the way, it is but Apocrypha) woman is resolved stronger than wine, yet whether it will be so or not, when wit is joined to it, may prove a fresh question.

Marrying, as our friend the late ambassador hath wittily observed, would certainly cure it; but that is a kind of live pigeons laid to the soles of the feet, a last remedy, and, to say truth, worse than the disease.

But, Jack, I remember I promised you a letter, not a treaty.[1] I now expect you should be just; and as I have showed you how to get out of love, so you, according to our bargain, should teach me how to get into it. I know you have but one way, and will prescribe me not to look upon Mistress Howard; but for that I must tell you aforehand that it is in love as in antipathy—the capers which will make my Lord of Dorset go from the table, another man will eat up. And, Jack, if you would make a visit to Bedlam, you shall find that there are rarely two there mad for the same thing.—Your humble servant.

Though, madam, I have ever hitherto believed play to be a thing in itself as merely indifferent as religion to a statesman or love made in a privy-chamber; yet hearing you have resolved it otherwise for me, my faith shall alter without becoming more learned upon it, or once knowing why it should do so. So great and just a sovereignty is that your reason hath above all others, that mine must be a rebel to itself, should it not obey thus easily; and, indeed, all the infallibility of judgment we poor Protestants have, is at this time wholly in your hands.

The loss of a mistress (which kills men only in

---

[1] [Treatise.]

romances, and is still digested with the first meat we eat after it) had yet in me raised up so much passion, and so just a quarrel, as I thought, to fortune for it, that I could not but tempt her to do me right upon the first occasion; yet, madam, has it not made me so desperate, but that I can sit down a loser both of that, time and money too, when there shall be the least fear of losing you.

And now, since I know your ladyship is too wise to suppose to yourself impossibilities, and therefore cannot think of such a thing as of making me absolutely good, it will not be without some impatience that I shall attend to know what sin you will be pleased to assign me in the room of this : something that has less danger about it, I conceive it would be; and therefore, if you please, madam, let it not be women, for, to say truth, it is a diet I cannot yet relish, otherwise than men do that on which they surfeited last.—Your humblest servant,

J. S.

[*To Aglaura* (?)]

MADAM,—Before this instant I did not believe Warwickshire the other world, or that Milcot walks had been the Blessed Shades. At my arrival here I am saluted by all as risen from the dead, and have had joy given me preposterously and as impertinently as they give it to men who marry where they do not love. If I should now die in earnest, my friends have nothing to pay me, for they have discharged the rites of funeral sorrow beforehand. Nor do I take it ill that report, which made Richard the Second alive so often after he was dead, should kill me as often when I am alive. The advantage is on my side. The only quarrel I have is, that they have made use of the whole "Book of Martyrs" upon me ; and without all question, the first Christians under the great persecutions suffered not in 500 years so many several ways as I have done in six days in this lewd town. This, madam, may seem strange unto you now, who know the company I was in ; and certainly, if at that time I had departed this transitory world, it had been a way they had never thought on, and this epitaph of the Spaniard's (changing the names) would better have become my gravestone than any other my friends the poets would have found out for me :—

Epitaph.

Here lies Don Alonzo,
Slain by a wound received under
His left pap,
The orifice of which was so
Small, no chirurgeon could
Discover it.
Reader,
If thou wouldest avoid so strange
A death,
Look not upon Lucinda's eyes.

Now all this discourse of dying, madam, is but to let you know how dangerous a thing it is to be long from London, especially in a place which is concluded out of the world. If you are not to be frightened hither, I hope you are to be persuaded ; and if good sermons or good plays, new braveries or fresh wit, revels, madam, masques that are to be, have any rhetoric about them, here they are, I assure you, in perfection, without asking leave of the provinces beyond seas, or the assent of ——. I write not this that you should think I value these pleasures above those of Milcot; for I must here protest, I prefer the single tabor and pipe in the great hall far above them; and were there no more belonging to a journey than riding so many miles, would my affairs conspire with my desires, your ladyship should find there, not at the bottom of a letter, Madam, your humble servant.

[To Lady Southcot.]

MADAM,—I thank heaven we live in an age in which the widows wear colours, and in a country where the women that lose their husbands [1] may be trusted with poison, knives, and all the burning coals in Europe, notwithstanding the president [2] of Sophonisba and Portia. Considering the estate you are in now, I should reasonably imagine meaner physicians than Seneca or Cicero might administer comfort. It is so far from me to imagine this accident should surprise you, that, in my opinion, it should not make you wonder, it being not strange at all that a man who hath lived ill all his time in a house should break a window, or steal away in the night through an unusual postern. You are now free; and what matter is it to a prisoner whether the fetters be taken off the ordinary way or not? If instead of putting off handsomely the chain of matrimony he hath rudely broke it, 'tis at his own charge; nor should it cost you a tear. Nothing,

---

[1] [Though without superscription of any kind in the original copies, it is clear, from internal evidence, that this letter was written by Suckling to his sister Martha, and just after the receipt of the news that her husband had deserted her.]

[2] [Precedent.]

madam, has worse mien [1] than counterfeit sorrow; and you must have the height of woman's art to make you appear other, especially when the spectators shall consider all the story.

The sword that was [2] placed betwixt a contracted princess and an ambassador was as much a husband; and the only difference was that that sword, laid in bed, allowed one to supply its place. This husband denied all, like a false crow [3] set up in a garden, which keeps others from the fruit it cannot taste itself. I would not have you so much as inquire, whether it were with his garters or his cloak-bag strings, nor engage yourself to fresh sighs by hearing new relations.

The Spanish princess Leonina, whom Balzac delivers the ornament of the last age, was wise, who, hearing a post was sent to tell her husband was dead, and knowing the secretary was in the way for that purpose, sent to stay the post till the arrival of the secretary, that she might not be obliged to shed tears twice. Of all things, the less we know the better. Curiosity would here be as vain as if a cuckold should inquire whether it were upon the couch or a bed, and whether the cavalier pulled off his spurs first or not.

I must confess it is a just subject for our sorrow to hear of any that does quit his station without his leave that placed him there; [4] and yet, as ill a mien as this act has, 'twas *a-la-Romansci*, as you may see by a line of Master Shakespeare's who, bringing in Titinius after a lost battle, speaking to his sword, and bidding it find out his heart, adds—

" By your leave, gods, this is a Roman's part." [5]

---

[1] [Old copies, *mine.*]   [2] [Old copies, *is.*]
[3] [A scarecrow.]
[4] [How sadly this passage, and how strangely too, reads by the side of the catastrophe which deprived the world so prematurely of the writer of it!]   [5] ["Julius Cæsar," act v, sc. 3]

'Tis true, I think, cloak-bag strings were not then so much in fashion ; but to those that are not sword-men the way is not so despicable ; and, for mine own part, I assure you Christianity highly governs me in the minute in which I do not wish with all my heart, that all the discontents in his majesty's three kingdoms would find out this very way of satisfying themselves and the world. J. S.

Sir,—Since the settling of your family would certainly much conduce to the settling of your mind, the care of the one being the trouble of the other, I cannot but reckon it in the number of my misfortunes that my affairs deny me the content I should take to serve you in it.

It would be too late now for me, I suppose, to advance or confirm you in those good resolutions I left you in, being confident your own reason hath been so just to you as long before this to have repre-sented a necessity of redeeming time and fame, and of taking a handsome revenge upon yourself for the injuries you would have done yourself.

Change, I confess, to them that think all at once, must needs be strange, and to you hateful, whom first your own nature, and then custom, another nature, have brought to delight in those narrow and uncouth [1] ways we found you in. You must there-fore consider that you have entered into one of those near conjunctions of which death is the only honour-able divorce, and that you have now to please another as well as yourself, who, though she be a woman, and by the patent she hath from nature hath

---

[1] [Little known, obscure.]

liberty to do simply, yet can she never be so strongly bribed against herself as to betray at once all her hopes and ends, and for your sake resolve to live miserably. Examples of such loving folly our times afford but few; and in those there are, you shall find the stock of love to have been greater, and their strengths richer to maintain it, than [it] is to be feared yours can be.

Woman, besides the trouble, has ever been thought a rent-charge; and though through the vain curiosity of man it has often been enclosed, yet has it seldom been brought to improve or become profitable. It faring with married men for the most part as with those that at great charges wall in grounds and plant, who cheaper might have eaten melons elsewhere, than in their own gardens cucumbers. The ruins that either time, sickness, or the melancholy you shall give her, shall bring, must all be made up at your cost; for that thing a husband is but tenant for life in what he holds, and is bound to leave the place tenantable to the next that shall take it. To conclude, a young woman is a hawk upon her wings; and if she be handsome, she is the more subject to go out at check. Falconers, that can but seldom spring right game, should still have something about them to take them down with. The lure to which all stoop in this world is either garnished with profit or pleasure; and when you cannot throw her the one, you must be content to show out the other. This I speak not out of a desire to increase your fears, which are already but too many, but out of a hope that, when you know the worst, you will at once leap into the river, and swim through handsomely, and not, weatherbeaten with the divers blasts of irresolution, stand shivering upon the brink.

Doubts and fears are, of all, the sharpest passions, and are still turning distempers to diseases. Through these false optics 'tis, all that you see is, like evening shadows, disproportionable to the truth, and strangely longer than the true substance. These, when a handsome way of living, and expense suitable to your fortune, is represented to you, makes you in their stead see want and beggary, thrusting upon your judgment impossibilities for likelihoods, which they with ease may do, since, as Solomon saith, they betray the succours that reason offers.

'Tis true that all here below is but diversified folly, and that the little things we laugh at children for, we do but act ourselves in great; yet is there difference of lunacy; and, of the two, I had much rather be mad with him that, when he had nothing, thought all the ships that came into the haven his, than with you who, when you have so much coming in, think you have nothing. This fear of losing all in you is the ill issue of a worse parent, desire of getting, in you; so that, if you would not be passion-rent, you must cease to be covetous. Money in your hand is like the conjuror's devil, which while you think you have, that has you.

The rich talent that God hath given, or rather lent, you, you have hid up in a napkin, and man knows no difference betwixt that and treasures kept by ill spirits, but that yours is the harder to come by. To the guarding of these golden apples of necessity must be kept those never-sleeping dragons, fear, jealousy, distrust, and the like; so that you are come to moralise Æsop, and his fables of beasts are become prophecies of you; for, while you have catched at the shadow, uncertain riches, you have lost the substance, true content.

The desire I have ye should be yet yourself, and that your friends should have occasion to bless the providence of misfortune, has made me take the boldness to give you your own character, and to show you yourself out of your own glass; and though all this tells you but where you are [hurt], yet it is some part of a cure to have search'd the wound, and for this time we must be content to do like travellers, who first find out the place, and then the nearest way.

———

My noble Lord,—Your humble servant had the honour to receive from your hand a letter, and had the grace upon the sight of it to blush. I but then found my own negligence, and but now could have the opportunity to ask pardon for it. We have ever since been upon a march, and the places we are come to have afforded rather blood than ink; and of all things, sheets have been the hardest to come by, specially those of paper. If these few lines shall have the happiness to kiss your hand, they can assure that he that sent them knows none to whom he owes more obligation than to your lordship, and to whom he would more willingly pay it; and that it must be no less than necessity itself that can hinder him from often presenting it. Germany hath no whit altered me; I am still the humble servant of my Lord —— that I was, and when I cease to be so, I must cease to be   John Suckling.

———

[To Aglaura.]

Since you can breathe no one desire that was not mine before it was yours, or full as soon (for hearts united never knew divided wishes), I must chide you,

dear princess, not thank you, for your present; and
(if at least I knew how) be angry with you for sending
him a blush, who needs must blush because you sent
him one.   If you are conscious of much, what am I
then, who guilty am of all you can pretend to, and
something more—unworthiness.   But why should you
at all, heart of my heart, disturb the happiness you
have so newly given me, or make love feed on doubts,
that never yet could thrive on such a diet?   *If I have
granted your request!*   O, why will you ever say that
you have studied me, and give so great an interest to
the contrary!   That wretched *if* speaks as if I would
refuse what you desire, or could—both which are
equally impossible.   My dear princess, there needs no
new approaches where the breach is made already;
nor must you ever ask anywhere, but of your fair self,
for anything that shall concern your humble servant.

[*To the same.*]

My dearest Princess,—But that I know I love
you more than ever any did any, and that yet I hate
myself, because I can love you no more, I should now
most unsatisfied despatch away this messenger.

The little that I can write to what I would, makes
me think writing a dull commerce, and then—how
can I choose but wish myself with you—to say the
rest.   My dear dear, think what merit, virtue, beauty:
what and how far Aglaura, with all her charms, can
oblige; and so far and something more I am, your
humble servant.

A letter to a friend[1] to dissuade him from marrying a widow which he formerly had been in love with, and quitted.

AT this time when no hot planet fires the blood, and when the lunatics of Bedlam themselves are trusted abroad, that you should run mad, is, sir, not so much a subject for your friends' pity as their wonder. 'Tis true, love is a natural distemper, a kind of small-pox. Every one either hath had it, or is to expect it—and the sooner the better.

Thus far you are excused. But having been well cured of a fever, to court a relapse, to make love the second time in the same place, is, not to flatter you, neither better nor worse than to fall into a quagmire by chance, and ride into it afterwards on purpose. 'Tis not love, Tom, that doth the mischief, but constancy; for love is of the nature of a burning-glass which, kept still in one place, fireth; changed often, it doth nothing—a kind of glowing coal which, with shifting from hand to hand, a man easily endures. But then

An answer to the letter.

CEASE to wonder, honest Jack, and give me leave to pity thee, who labourest to condemn that which thou confessest natural, and the sooner had the better.

Thus far there needs no excuse, unless it be on thy behalf, who stylest second thoughts (which are by all allowed the best), a relapse, and talkest of a quagmire where no man ever stuck fast, and accuseth constancy of mischief in what is natural and advisedly undertaken.

'Tis confessed that love changed often doth nothing —nay, 'tis nothing ; for love and change are incompatible ; but where it is kept fixed to its first object, though it burn not, yet it warms and cherisheth ; so as it needs no transplantation or change of soil to make it fruitful ; and certainly, if love be natural, to marry is the best recipe for living honest.

Yes, I know what marriage is, and know you know it not, by terming it the dearest way of curing love ; for certainly there goes more charge to the keeping of a stable full of horses,

---

[1] [Thomas Carew.]

to marry, Tom ! Why, thou hadst better to live honest. Love, thou knowest is blind; what will he do when he hath fetters on, thinkest thou ?

Dost thou know what marriage is ? "Tis curing of love the dearest way, or waking a losing gamester out of a winning dream, and after a long expectation of a strange banquet, a presentation of a homely meal. Alas ! Tom, love seeds when it runs up to matrimony, and is good for nothing. Like some fruittrees, it must be transplanted, if thou wouldst have it active, and bring forth anything.

Thou now perchance hast vow'd all that can be vowed to any one face, and thinkest thou hast left nothing unsaid to it ; do but make love to another, and if thou art not suddenly furnished with new language and fresh oaths, I will conclude Cupid hath used thee worse than ever he did any of his train.

After all this, to marry a widow, a kind of chewed meat ! What a fantastical stomach hast thou, that canst not eat of a dish till another man hath cut of it ?

than one only steed ; and much of vanity is therein besides, when, be the errand what it will, this one steed shall serve your turn as well as twenty more. O, if you could serve your steed so !

Marriage turns pleasing dreams to ravishing realities, which out-do what fancy or expectation can frame unto themselves.

That love doth seed when it runs into matrimony, is undoubted truth ; how else should it increase and multiply, which is its greatest blessing.

'Tis not the want of love, nor Cupid's fault, if every day afford not new language and new ways of expressing affection ; it rather may be caused through an excess of joy, which oftentimes strikes dumb.

These things considered, I will marry ; nay, and to prove the second paradox false, I'll marry a widow, who is rather the chewer, than thing chewed. How strangely fantastical is he who will be an hour in plucking on a strait boot,[1] when he may be forthwith furnished with enough that will come on easily, and do him as much credit and

---

[1] [A pleasant thrust at the boots Suckling affected.]

Who would wash after another, when he might have fresh water enough for asking.

Life is sometimes a long journey. To be tied to ride upon one beast still, and that half tired to thy hand too! Think upon that, Tom.

Well, if thou must needs marry (as who can tell to what height thou hast sinned), let it be a maid, and no widow; for, as a modern author hath wittily resolved in this case, 'tis better, if a man must be in prison, to lie in a private room than in the hole.

better service? Wine, when first broached, drinks not half so well as after a while drawing. Would you not think him a madman who, whilst he might fair and easily ride on the beaten roadway, should trouble himself with breaking up of gaps? A well-wayed horse will safely convey thee to thy journey's end, when an unbacked filly may by chance give thee a fall. 'Tis prince-like to marry a widow, for 'tis to have a taster.

'Tis true, life may prove a long journey; and so, believe me, it must do. A very long one too, before the beast you talk of prove tired. Think you upon that, Jack.

Thus, Jack, thou seest my well-ta'en resolution of marrying, and that a widow, not a maid; to which I am much induced out of what Pythagoras saith, in his 2d sect. "Cuniculorum," that it is better lying in the hole than sitting in the stocks.

[*To Aglaura.*]

WHEN I receive your lines, my dear princess, and find there expressions of a passion, though reason and my own immerit tell me it must not be for me, yet is the cosenage so pleasing to me, that I, bribed

by my own desires, believe them still before the
other. Then do I glory that my virgin-love has
stayed for such an object to fix upon, and think how
good the stars were to me that kept me from quenching those flames youth or wild love furnished me
withal in common and ordinary waters, and reserved
me a sacrifice for your eyes. While thought thus
smiles and solaces himself within me, cruel remembrance breaks in upon our retirements, and tells so
sad a story that, trust me, I forget all that pleased
fancy said before, and turn[1] my thoughts to where I
left you. Then I consider that storms neither know
courtship nor pity, and that those rude blasts will
often make you a prisoner this winter, if they do no
worse.

While I here enjoy fresh diversion, you make the
sufferings more by having leisure to consider them;
nor have I now any way left me to make mine equal
with them, but by often considering that they are not
so; for the thought that I cannot be with you to bear
my share is more intolerable to me than if I had
borne more. But I was only born to number hours,
and not enjoy them; yet can I never think myself
unfortunate, while I can write myself Aglaura her
humble servant.

[*To the same.*]

WHEN I consider, my dear princess, that I have no
other pretence to your favours than that which all
men have to the original of beauty, light, which we
enjoy, not that 'tis the inheritance of our eyes, but
because things most excellent cannot restrain themselves, but are ours, as they are diffusively good; then

---

[1] [Old copies, *turnes.*]

do I find the justness of your quarrel, and cannot but blush to think what I do owe, but much more to think what I do pay, since I have made the principal so great, by sending in so little interest.

When you have received this humble confession, you will not, I hope, conceive me one that would, though upon your bidding, enjoy myself, while there is such a thing in the world as Aglaura.—Her humble servant,   J. S.

[*To the same.*]

So much, dear ——, was I ever yours, since I had first the honour to know you, and consequently so little myself, since I had the unhappiness to part with you, that you yourself, dear, without what I would say, cannot but have been so just as to have imagined the welcome of your own letters ; though indeed they have but removed me from one rack to set me on another —from fears and doubts I had about me of your welfare to an unquietness within myself, till I have deserved this intelligence.

How pleasingly troublesome thought and remembrance have been to me, since I left you, I am no more able now to express, than another to have them so. You only could make every place you came in worth the thinking of; and I do think those places worthy my thought only, because you made them so. But I am to leave them, and I shall do't the willinger, because the gamester still is so much in me, as that I love not to be told too often of my losses. Yet every place will be alike, since every good object will do the same. Variety of beauty and of faces, quick underminers of constancy to others, to me will be but pillars to support it, since, when they please me most, I most shall think of you.

In spite of all philosophy, it will be hottest in my climate when my sun is farthest off; and in spite of all reason, I proclaim that I am not myself, but when I am yours wholly.

[*To the same.*]

THOUGH desire, in those that love, be still like too much sail in a storm, and man cannot so easily strike, or take all in when he pleases ; yet, dearest princess, be it never so hard, when you shall think it dangerous, I shall not make it difficult ; though—well, love is love, and air is air ; and, though you are a miracle yourself, yet do not I believe that you can work any. Without it I am confident you can never make these two, thus different in themselves, one and the selfsame thing ; when you shall, it will be some small furtherance towards it, that you have your humble servant, J. S.

Whoso truly loves the fair Aglaura, that he will never know desire, at least not entertain it, that brings not letters of recommendation from her, or first a fair passport.

[*To the same.*]

MY DEAR DEAR,—Think I have kissed your letter to nothing, and now know not what to answer ; or that, now I am answering, I am kissing you to nothing, and know not how to go on ! For, you must pardon, I must hate all I send you here, because it expresses nothing in respect of what it leaves behind with me. And O ! why should I write then ? Why should I not come myself? Those tyrants, business, honour, and necessity, what have they to do with you and I? Why should we not do love's commands before theirs, whose sovereignty is but usurped upon us? Shall we not smell to roses 'cause others do look on, or gather them 'cause there are prickles, and something that would hinder us? Dear, I fain would, and know no hindrance but what must come from you; and why should any come? since 'tis not I, but you, must be sensible how much time we lose, it being long time since I was not myself, but yours.

———

[*To the same.*]

DEAR PRINCESS,—Finding the date of your letter so young, and having an assurance from ——— who at the same time heard from Master ——— that all our letters have been delivered at B———,[1] I cannot but imagine some ill mistake, and that you have not received any at all. Faith, I have none in Welshman;[2] and though fear and suspicion look often so far that they oversee the right, yet, when love holds the candle, they seldom do mistake so much. My dearest princess, I shall long, next hearing you are well, to hear that they are safe; for though I can never be ashamed to be found an idolater to such a shrine as yours, yet since the world is full of profane eyes, the best way, sure, is to keep all mysteries from them, and to let privacy be (what indeed it is) the best part of devotion. So thinks, my D. D. P. Your humble servant.

---

[1] [Query, Baron-Hill. See a note *post.*]
[2] [A Welshman employed as a messenger.]

[*To the same.*]

SINCE the inferior orbs move but by the first,[1] without all question desires and hopes in me are to be governed still by you, as they by it. What mean these fears, then, dear princess?

Though planets wander, yet is the sphere that carries them the same still; and though wishes in me may be extravagant, yet he in whom they make their motion is, you know, my dear princess, yours, and wholly to be disposed of by you.

And till we hear from you, though, according to the form of concluding a letter, we should now rest, we cannot.

[*To the same.*]

FAIR PRINCESS,—If parting be a sin, as sure it is, what then to part from you? If to extenuate an ill be to increase it, what then now to excuse it by letter? That which we would allege to lessen it, with you perchance has added to the guilt already, which is our sudden leaving you. Abruptness is an eloquence in parting, when spinning out of time is but the weaving of new sorrow. And thus we thought; yet being not all able to distinguish of our own acts, the fear we may have sinned farther than we think of has made us send to you to know whether it be mortal or not.

---

[1] [*i.e.*, The primary orb.]

For the two Excellent Sisters.[1]

THOUGH I conceive you, ladies, so much at leisure
that you may read anything, yet since the stories of
the town are merely amorous, and sound nothing but
love, I cannot, without betraying my own judgment,
make them news for Wales.   Nor can it be less im-
proper to transport them to you, than for the king to
send my Lord of C—— over ambassador this winter
into Greenland.

It would want faith in so cold a country as Anglesey
to say that your Cousin Duchess, for the quenching of
some foolish flames about her, has endured quietly
the loss of much of the king's favour, of many of her
houses, and of most of her friends.

Whether the disfigurement that travel or sickness
has bestowed upon B. W—— be thought so great by
the Lady of the Isle as 'tis by others, and whether the
alteration of his face has bred a change in her mind,
it never troubles you, ladies, what old loves are
decayed, or what new ones are sprung up in their
room.   Whether this lady be too discreet, or that
cavalier not secret enough, are things that concern
the inhabitants of Anglesey not at all.   A fair day is
better welcome and more news than all that can be
said in this kind ; and for all that I know now, the
devil's chimney is on fire, or his pot seething over,
and all North Wales not able to stay the fury of it.
Perchance, while I write this, a great black cloud is
sailing from Mistress Thomas's bleak mountains over

---

[1] [Probably Aglaura and her sister.]

to Baron-Hill,[1] there to disgorge itself with what the sea or worse places fed it with before.

It may be, the honest banks about you turn bankrupt too, and break ; and the sea, like an angry creditor, seizes upon all, and hath no pity, because he has been put off so long from time to time. For variety (and it is not impossible), some boisterous wind flings up the hangings ; and thinking to do as much to your clothes, finds a resistance, and so departs, but first breaks all the windows about the house for it in revenge.

These things, now, we that live in London cannot help, and they are as great news to men that sit in boxes at Blackfriars, as the affairs of love to flannel weavers.

For my own part, I think I have made a great compliment when I have wished myself with you, and more than I dare make good in winter ; and yet there is none would venture farther for such a happiness than your humble servant.

The Wine-drinkers to the Water-drinkers, greeting :

WHEREAS, by your ambassador, two days since sent unto us, we understand that you have lately had a plot to surprise, or, to speak more properly, to take the waters, and in it have not only a little miscarried,

---

[1] [In Beaumaris, the seat of Sir Richard Bulkeley, son of a father of both his names, who was Elizabeth's favourite. Baron-Hill was built (Pennant's "Tours in Wales," 1810, iii. 42) by Sir Richard in 1618. The *B. W.* above mentioned may represent the inverted initials of one of the same family. The *B*—— referred to in a former letter is doubtless Baron-Hill.]

but also met with such difficulties that, unless you be speedily relieved, you are like to suffer in the adventure. We, as well out of pity to you as out of care to our state and commonwealth (knowing that women have ever been held necessary, and that nothing relisheth so well after wine), have so far taken it into our consideration, that we have neglected no means, since we heard of it first, that might be for your contents or the good of the cause ; and therefore to that purpose we have had divers meetings at the Bear at the Bridge-foot, and now at length have resolved to despatch to you one of our cabinet council, Colonel Young, with some slight forces of canary, and some few of sherry, which no doubt will stand you in good stead, if they do not mutiny and grow too headstrong for their commander. Him Captain Puff of Barton shall follow with all expedition, with two or three regiments of claret ; Monsieur de Granville, commonly called Lieutenant Strutt, shall lead up the rear of Rhenish and white. These succours, thus timely sent, we are confident will be sufficient to hold the enemy in play, and, till we hear from you again, we shall not think of a fresh supply. For the waters (though perchance they have driven you into some extremities, and divers times forc'd their passages through some of your best-guarded places), yet have they, if our intelligence fail us not, hitherto had the worst of it still, and evermore at length plainly run away from you.

Given under our hands at the Bear, this fourth of July.

Since joy, the thing we all so court, is but our hopes stripped of our fears, pardon me if I be still

pressing at it, and, like those that are curious to know
their fortunes aforehand, desire to be satisfied, though
it displeases me afterward. To this gentleman (who
has as much insight as the t'other wanted eyesight)
I have committed the particulars, which would too
much swell a letter. If they shall not please you, 'tis
but fresh subject still for repentance, nor ever did that
make me quarrel with anything but my own stars.
To swear new oaths from this place were but to
weaken the credit of those I have sworn in another.
If heaven be to forgive you now for not believing of
them then, as sure as it was a sin, heaven forgive me
now for swearing of them then, for that was double
sin.   More than I am I cannot be, nor list, yours,

J. S.

I am not so ill a Protestant as to believe in merit,
yet if you please to give answer under your own
hand, such as I shall for ever rely upon, if I have not
deserved it already, it is not impossible but I may.

———

*To a Cousin, who still loved young girls, and when they
came to be marriageable, quitted them, and fell in
love with fresh, at his father's request, who desired
he might be persuaded out of the humour, and
marry.*[1]

Honest Charles,—Were there not fools enou'
before in the commonwealth of lovers, but that thou
must bring up a new sect? Why delighted with the
first knots of roses ; and when they come to blow, can

---

[1] [This is the letter to Charles Suckling mentioned in the
Memoir.]

satisfy the sense, and do the end of their creation, dost not care for them? Is there nothing in this foolish transitory world that thou canst find out to set thy heart upon, but that which has newly left off making of dirt-pies, and is but preparing itself for loam and a green sickness? Seriously, Charles, and without ceremony, 'tis very foolish, and to love widows is as tolerable an humour, and as justifiable as thine; for beasts that have been rid off their legs are as much for a man's use as colts that are unwayed, and will not go at all. Why the devil such young things? Before these understand what thou wouldst have, others would have granted. Thou dost not marry them neither, nor anything else. 'Sfoot, it is the story of the jackanapes and the partridges: thou starest after a beauty till it is lost to thee; and then lett'st out another, and starest after that till it is gone too! Never considering that it is here as in the Thames, and that while it runs up in the middle, it runs down on the sides; while thou contemplatest the coming-in-tide and flow of beauty, that it ebbs with thee, and that thy youth goes out at the same time. After all this, too, she thou now art cast upon will have much ado to avoid being ugly. Pox on't, men will say thou wert benighted, and wert glad of any inn. Well, Charles, there is another way, if you could find it out. Women are like melons—too green or too ripe are worth nothing—you must try till you find a right one. Taste all—but hark you, Charles, you shall not need to eat of all; for one is sufficient for a surfeit.—Your most humble servant.

I should have persuaded you to marriage; but, to deal ingenuously, I am a little out of arguments that way at this present. 'Tis honourable, there's no question on't; but what more, in good faith, I cannot readily tell.

MADAM,—To tell you that neither my misfortunes nor my sins did draw from me ever so many sighs as my departure from you has done, and that there are yet tears in mine eyes left undried for it : or that melancholy has so deeply seized me, that colds and diseases hereafter shall not need above half their force to destroy me, would be, I know, superfluous and vain, since so great a goodness as yours cannot but have out-believed already what I can write.

He never knew you that will not think the loss of your company greater than the Imperialists can all this time the loss of all their companies ; and he shall never know you that can think it greater than I who, though I never had any wisdom, nor wit enough to admire you to your worth, yet had my judgment ever so much right in it as to admire you above all. And thus he says that dares swear he is your most devoted servant.

MADAM,—The distrust I have had of not being able to write to you anything which might pay the charge of reading, has persuaded me to forbear kissing your hands at this distance. So, like women that grow proud because they are chaste, I thought I might be negligent because I was not troublesome ; and were I not safe in your goodness, I should be, madam, in your judgment, which is too just to value little observances, or think them necessary to the right honouring my [1] lady.

Your ladyship, I make no doubt, will take into consideration that superstition hath ever been fuller of ceremony than the true worship. When it shall

---

[1] [Perhaps *any.*]

O

concern any part of your real service, and I not throw by all respects whatsoever to manifest my devotion, take what revenge you please. Undo me, madam; resume my best place and title, and let me be no longer your humble servant.

MADAM,—By the same reason the ancients made no sacrifice to death, should your ladyship send me no letters, since there has been no return on my side. But the truth is, the place affords nothing: all our days are (as the women here) alike, and the difference of Fair does rarely show itself. Such great state do beauty and the sun keep in these parts. I keep company with my own horses, madam, to avoid that of the men; and by this you may guess how great an enemy to my living contentedly my lady is, whose conversation has brought me to so fine a diet that, wheresoever I go, I must starve: all days are tedious, companies troublesome, and books themselves (feasts heretofore) no relish in them. Finding you to be the cause of all this, excuse me, madam, if I resent, and continue peremptory in the resolution I have taken to be, madam, during life your humblest servant.

MADAM,—But that I know your goodness is not mercenary, and that you receive thanks either with as much trouble as men ill news, or with as much wonder as virgins unexpected love, this letter should be full of them. A strange, proud return you may think I make you, madam, when I tell you, it is not from everybody I would be thus obliged; and that, if I thought you did me not these favours because you love me, I should not love you, because you do me these favours. This is not language for one in affliction, I confess, and upon whom, it may be, at this present a cloud is breaking; but finding not within myself I have deserved that storm, I will not make it greater by apprehending it.

After all, lest, madam, you should think I take your favours as tribute, to my own great grief I here declare, that the services I shall be able to render you will be no longer presents, but payments of debts, since I can do nothing for you hereafter which I was not obliged to do before. Madam, your most humble and faithful servant.

MY NOBLE FRIEND,—That you have overcome the danger of the land and of the sea is news most welcome to us, and with no less joy received amongst us than if the King of Sweden had the second time overcome Tilly, and again passed the Maine and the Rhine. Nor do we in this look more upon ourselves and private interests than on the public, since in your safety both were comprised ; and though you had not had about you the affairs and secrets of state, yet to have left your own person upon the way had been half to undo our poor island, and the loss must have been lamented with the tears of a whole kingdom.

But you are now beyond all our fears, and have nothing to take heed on yourself but fair ladies. A pretty point of security, and such a one as all Germany cannot afford. We here converse with northern beauties, that had never heat enough to kindle a spark in any man's breast, where heaven had been first so merciful as to put in a reasonable soul.

There is nothing either fair or good in this part of the world, and I cannot name the thing can give me any content, but the thought that you enjoy enough otherwhere. I having ever been, since I had the first honour to know you, yours more than his own.

———

My Lord,—To persuade one that has newly ship-wrecked upon a coast to embark suddenly for the same place again, or your lordship to seek that content you now enjoy in the innocence of a solitude among the disorders and troubles of a court, were, I think, a thing the king himself (and majesty is no ill orator) would find some difficulty to do ; and yet, when I consider that great soul of yours, like a spider, working all inwards, and sending forth nothing but, like the cloistered schoolmen's divinity, threads fine and unprofitable—if I thought you would not suspect my being serious all this while, for what I should now say, I would tell you that I cannot but be as bold with you as your ague is, and for a little time, whether you will or not, entertain you scurvily.

When I consider you look (to me) like ——, I cannot but think it as odd a thing as if I should see Vandyke with all his fine colours and pencils about him, his frame and right light, and everything in order, and yet his hands tied behind him ; and your lordship must excuse me, if upon it I be as bold.

The wisest men and greatest states have made no scruple to make, use of brave men whom they had laid by with some disgrace ; nor have those brave men, so laid by, made scruple, or thought it a disgrace, to serve again when they were called to it afterwards.

These general motives of the state and common good I will not so much as once offer up to your

lordship's consideration, though, as 'tis fit, they have
still the upper end. Yet, like great aloes,[1] they
rather make a show than provoke appetite. There
are two things which I shall not be ashamed to propound to you as ends, since the greater part of the
wise men of the world have not been ashamed to
make them theirs, and, if any has been found to contemn them, it hath been strongly to be suspected
that either they could not easily attain to them, or
else that the readiest way to attain to them was to
contemn them. These two are honour and wealth ;
and though you stand possessed of both of them, yet
is the first in your hands like a sword which, if not
through negligence, by mischance hath taken rust,
and needs a little clearing, and it would be much
handsomer a present to posterity, if you yourself in
your lifetime wipe it off.

For your estate (which, it may be, had been more,
had it not been so much), though it is true that it is
so far from being contemptible that it is nobly com-
petent, yet must it be content to undergo the same
fate greater estates (commonwealths themselves) have
been and are subject to ; which is, when it comes to
be divided in itself, not to be considerable. Both
honour and estate are too fair and sweet flowers to
be without prickles, or to be gathered without some
scratches.

And now, my lord, I know you have nothing to
urge but a kind of incapability in yourself to the
service of this state, when indeed you have made the
only bar you have by imagining you have one.

I confess, though, had vice so large an empire in
the court as heretofore it has had, or were the times
so dangerous that to the living well there wise conduct were more necessary than virtue itself, your

---

[1] [Suckling employs this figure in " Brennoralt," act ii. sc. 1.]

lordship would have reason, with Æsop's country
mouse, to undervalue all change of condition, since
a quiet mediocrity is still to be preferred before a
troubled superfluity. But these things are now no
more ; and if at any time they have threatened that
horizon, like great clouds, either they are fallen of
themselves to the ground, or else, upon the appearing
of the sun, such a prince as ours is, they have
vanished, and left behind them clear and fair days.
To descend to parts, envy is so lessened, that it is
almost lost into virtuous emulation, every man [1]
trusting the king's judgment so far, that he knows no
better measure of his own merit than his reward.
The little word behind the back and undoing whisper
which, like pulling of a sheet-rope at sea, slackens the
sail, and makes the gallantest ship stand still; that
heretofore made the faulty and the innocent alike
guilty, is a thing, I believe, now so forgot, or at least
so unpractised, that those that are the worst have
leisure to grow good before any will take notice they
have been otherwise, or at least divulge it.

'Tis true, faction there is ; but 'tis as true, that it is,
as the winds are, to clear and keep places free from
corruption, the oppositions being as harmless as that
of the meeting tides under the bridge, whose encounter
makes it but more easy for him that is to pass. To
be a little pleasant in my instances : the very women
have suffered reformation, and wear through the
whole court their faces as little disguised now as an
honest man's actions should be ; and if there be any
have suffered themselves to be gained by their servants, their ignorance of what they granted may well
excuse them from the shame of what they did. So
that it is more than possible to be great and good ;
and we may safely conclude, if there be some that

---

[1] [Old copy, *mans.*]

are not so exact, as much as they fall short of it just so much they have gone from the great original, God, and from the best copies of him on earth, the king and the queen.

To conclude : if those accidents or disasters which make men grow less in the world (as some such, my lord, have happened to you) were inevitable as death, or, when they were once entered upon us, there were no cure for them, examples of others would satisfy me for yours ; but since there have been that have delivered themselves from their ills, either by their good fortune or virtue, 'twould trouble me that my friends should not be found in that number, as much as if one should bring me a catalogue of those that truly honoured my Lord of ——, and I should not find among the first your humble servant.[1]

————

My Lord,[2]—But that you do and say things in Scotland now, my lord, unfit for a good subject to hear, I should have hoped your lordship, by a true relation of the passages there, would have disabused your humble servant here. Distance and men's fears have so enlarged the truth, and so disproportioned everything about the town, that we have made the little troop of discontents a gallant army, and already measure no Scotchman but by his evening shadow.

We hear say you have taken livery and seisin of

————

[1] [This letter is followed in the editions of 1646–48 by the epistle to Henry Jermyn, which now stands by itself, taken from the edition of 1641. See *post.*]

[2] [This and the following letters first appeared in the edition of 1658.]

Northumberland, and there are that give in Cumberland for quietness' sake, and are content to think it part of Scotland, because it is so barren. London scriveners begin to wish they had St Michael-Mount's-men's security for the borderers they have standing bound in their shops ; and the Witheringtons' and Howards' estates are already freely disposed to the needier rebels. Much of this part of the world is in agues, but not all, my lord ; there are that have read the chronicles, and they find the English oftener marched into Edinburgh than the Scots into London.

Your old friend, Alderman ——, a learned bard, and a great inseer into times, saith it is a boil broken out in the breech of the kingdom, and that when it is ripe, it will heal of itself. Others use a handsomer similitude, and compare Scotland to a hive of swarming bees which, they say, the king watches to reduce them for the better. There is a saucy kind of intelligence about the town, of ten thousand pounds that should be sent by my Lord M—— for redemption of affairs there ; but this the wiser sort suspects, for, besides that his majesty buys his own again, they say none but the king would give so much for it.

Some are scandalised at the word of union, and protest they find no resemblance betwixt this new covenant and our Saviour's. Others wonder why they would make use of religion rather than their poverty for the cause of their mutining, since the one is ever suspected, and the other none would have disputed.

In short, while one part of the town is in whisper and serious, the other part smiles. I therefore desire your lordship to send me word in what state things stand there, that I may know of which side to be. But I beseech you think it not any inbred love to mischief that I now send to inquire how rebellion prospers, but impute it to a certain foolish and greedy curiosity in man's nature of news, and remember that he that hath this disease about him is, your humble servant.

GOOD MASTER ALDERMAN,[1]—It is most true, I confess, that we do say things here unfit for you to hear there, and for this very reason I will forbear particulars. But this I do, Master Alderman, not so much out of fear for myself as care for you ; for though you write in the present tense, and use the particle *now*, which is a kind of an exclusive word, yet it is well enough known a Scotchman at all times might speak what an Englishman durst not hear. It seems, sir, strange to me, that in the beginning of your letter you give us the name of rebels, when none are more his majesty's most humble subjects than we, as in the front of our petitions and messages most plainly appears. True it is, that in case the king will not do what we would have him, we have provided arms, and have persuaded those here, and sent to others abroad to assist us ; but that we have at any time denied ourselves to be his most faithful subjects, by your favour, Master Alderman, I think will hardly appear. For the taking of livery and seisin of Northumberland, if there be any such thing, neither you nor my Lord —— ought to be troubled at it, for that is a business belongs to the law, and
- upon a trial had here in Edinburgh before any of the Covenant, no question but there will be a speedy end

---

[1] [This letter seems to have been written by Suckling in the character and name of a Scotish Covenanter, answering the imputations of a letter previously written by an English alderman —the same person to whom reference is made in the preceding epistle. Both that and the present were written in 1639.]

of it. The thing I most wonder at is, that our old friend should be so much mistaken as to call Scotland the breech of the kingdom, since you know that is a part of all the rest most subject, and is still put to endure the lash, so that in all likelihood it should rather be your country than ours.

For your simile of the bees, and reducing us to the better, you may assure his majesty from me that it will not quit cost ; for both his predecessors and himself have found sufficiently that, hived or unhived, we yield not much honey.

Now, sir, for our new Covenant's having relation to the other, you must know that, though it is not absolutely alike in all, yet in some things it doth not disagree, and in this especially it suits—that there is but little care taken for settling High Commission Courts in either.

The last scruple that troubles you is, why in this case we have made use of religion, which every one is apt to dispute, rather than poverty, which no man would have disputed ; and to say truth in this, I was something unsatisfied myself, until I had spoken with one of the learneder of the Covenant, who told me that he had observed very few to thrive by publishing their poverty, but a great many by pretending religion. And now I doubt not but I have in part satisfied your curiosity. There remains only that I give you my opinion concerning which party you ought to be of, and according to the friendship that is betwixt us, I will deal plainly with you, that if you had no more to lose than some of us have, this would be no ill side, for you see how God hath blessed the Hollanders. But, as you are, London is no ill place ; for, should you bring your money hither, the temptation would be too strong for the men, and like a hungry man brought to a strange table, we should fall to, without much inquiring whose the meat was.

An Answer to a Gentleman that sent to inquire after the Scottish business.[1]

SIR,—That you may receive an account of the Scottish business, and why there hath been such irresolution and alteration about the levies lately, it is fit you know that this northern storm, like a new disease, hath so far posed the doctors of state that as yet they have not given it a name, though perchance they all firmly believe it to be rebellion. And therefore, sir, it is no wonder if these do here as the learned in physic, who, when they know not certainly the grief, prescribe medicines sometimes too strong, sometimes too weak. The truth is, we here consider the Scottish affair much after the rate the mortals do the moon : the simpler think it no bigger than a bushel, and some (too wise) imagine it a vast world, with strange things undiscovered in it—certainly two ill ways of casting it up, since the first would make us too secure, the other too fearful. I confess, I know not how to meet it in the middle, or set it right ; nor do I think you have, since I should believe the question to be rather a king or no king there, than a bishop or no bishop. In great mutinies or insurrections of this nature pretentions speciously conscionable were never wanting, and indeed are necessary, for rebellion is itself so ugly, that did it not put on the vizard of religion, it would fright rather than draw people to it, and being drawn, it could not hold them without it.

Imaginary cords, that seem to fasten man to heaven, have tied things here below surer together than any

---

[1] [There is a copy of this letter in MS. Ashmole 826, art. 49.]

other obligation.[1]   If it be liberty of conscience they
ask, 'tis a foolish request, since they have it already,
and must have it in despite of power.   For, as
Theodoric the Goth said to the Jews, *Nemo cogitur
credere invitus.*   If the exercise of that liberty, 'tis
dangerous ; for not three men are of the same opinion
in all, and then each family must have a war within
itself.   Look upon their long preparations, and consider withal prophecy is ceased,[2] and therefore they
could not foretel this book should be sent unto them,
and you will conclude they rather employed Conscience than Conscience employed them.   Inquire
after their leaders, and you will hardly find them
apostles, or men of such sanctity that they should
order religion.   Lesley himself, if his story were
searched, would certainly be found one who, because
he could not live well there, took up a trade of killing
men abroad, and now is returned, for Christ's sake,
to kill men at home.   If you will have my opinion, I
think their quarrel to the king is that which they may
have to the sun : he doth not warm and visit them as
much as others.   God and nature have placed them
in the shade, and they are angry with the King of
England for it.   To conclude : this is the case.   The
great and wise Husbandman hath planted the beasts
in outfields, and they would break hedges to come
into the garden.   This is the belief of your humble
servant.

Sir,—We are at length arrived at that river[3] about
the uneven running of which my friend Master William

---

[1] [The Ashmole MS. reads—" Imaginary cords, that *seeke* to
tye man *and* heaven, *when as* they tye them surer below then
any obligation."]
[2] [So Ashmole MS.   Printed copies, *seal'd.*]
[3] [The Tweed.]

Shakespeare [1] makes Henry Hotspur quarrel so highly
with his fellow-rebels, and for his sake I have been
something curious to consider the scantlet of ground
that angry monsieur would have had in, but cannot
find it could deserve his choler, nor any of the other
side ours, did not the king think it did. The account
I shall now give you of the war will be but imperfect,
since I conceive it to be in the state that part of the
four and twenty hours is, in which we can neither call
night nor day. I should judge it dawning towards
earnest, did not the Lords Covenanters' letters to our
Lords here something divide me. So, sir, you may
now imagine us walking up and down the banks of
Tweed like the Tower lions in their cages, leaving
the people to think what we would do if we were let
loose. The enemy is not yet much visible. It may
be, it is the fault of the climate, which brings men as
slowly forwards as plants; but it gives us fears that
the men of peace will draw all this to a dumb-show,
and so destroy a handsome opportunity, which was
now offered, of producing glorious matter for future
chronicle.

These are but conjectures, sir. The last part of
my letter I reserve for a great and known truth, which
is, that I am, sir, your most humble servant, &c.

My Lord,—At this instant it is grown a calm
greater than the storm, and if you will believe the
soldier, worse. Good arms and horses are already
cheap, and there is nothing risen in value but a

---

[1] [An early instance of the use of a common modern collo-
quiism.

Scotchman. Whether it be, my lord, the word *native*, or the king's good nature, we know not ; but we find they really have that mercy on earth which we do but hope for from heaven ; nor can they sin so fast as they are forgiven.

Some, and not unreasonably perchance, will imagine that this may invite good subjects to be ill, and that, as the sun melts ice but hardens clay, majesty, when it softens rebellion, may make allegiance stubborn. If, my lord, they shall more straitly now besiege the king's ear, and more boldly engross suits, posterity must tell this miracle, that there went an army from the south, of which there was not one man lost, nor any man taken prisoner but the king.

All we have to raise the present joys above the future fears is, that we know majesty hath not swallowed down so severe pills as it was thought necessity would prescribe for the purging and setting itself right. Your humble servant.

———

Sir,—The little stops or progresses which either love of the public, private fears, niceties of honour, or jealousy have caused in the treaty now on foot, arrive at me so slowly, that unless I had one of Master Davenant's Barbary pigeons (and he now employs them all, he says, himself for the queen's use), I durst not venture to send them, sir, to you, lest, coming to your hands so late, you should call for the map to see whether my quarters were in England or in Barbary. The truth is, I am no first favourite to any Lord of Secrets at this time ; but when they come from Council, attend the short turn with those that are, and as in discharge of pieces, see a whisper go off some good space of time before I hear it, so satisfy my thirst of novelty from the stream, not from the fountain.

Our very thoughts are hardly news ; and while I now intend to write you other men's (for my own are not worthy of knowledge), it is not without some fear that they have already sent them to Whitehall them-selves.

There are, sir, here that have an opinion, necessity, not good nature, produced this treaty, and that the same necessity which made them thus wise for peace will make them as desperate for war, if it succeed not suddenly.

Some conceive little distrusts among themselves will facilitate the work, and that the danger, now grown nearer, will divide the body, by persuading each man to look to his own particular safety. So we see men in ships, while there is hope, assist each other ; but when the wreck grows visible, leave the common care, and consult only their own escape.

There are some imagine this treaty of either side is not so much to beget a good peace as a good cause, and that the subject could do no less than humbly petition, not to appear a rebel, nor the king no less than graciously to hear those petitions, not to appear a tyrant, and that when one party shall be found unreasonable, the other will be thought excusable.

J. S.

Sir,—I send to you now to know how we do here, for in my Lady Kent's [1] well-being much of ours consists. If I am the last, you must impute it to the tenderness of my fears, which durst not inquire into so great a

---

[1] [See " Inedited Poetical and Miscellanies," 1870, Notes.]

misfortune, or to the coming of bad news, which ever comes latest thither whither it knows it shall be most unwelcome. For I confess, the report of so great a sickness as my Lady Kent's would give me more trouble than half the sex, although amongst the rest a mistress or two took their fortunes ; and though such excellence cannot change but for the better, yet you must excuse us that enjoy the benefit of her conversation here, if we are content Heaven should only give her the blessing of the Old Testament, and for a while defer those of the New. The only comfort I have had in the midst of variety of reports hath been that I have seen nothing of extraordinary in the elements of late, and I conceived it but reasonable that so general an ill, as my Lady Kent's death would be, should be proclaimed by no less than what foretells the evil of great princes or the beginning of great plagues. When so unlucky a minute shall arrive, I would conclude the virtuous and better sort of people have lost some of their power and credit above, and that the sins are more particularly punished of him that is her much obliged, and, sir, your most humble servant, J. S.

LADIES,—The opinion of things is the measure of their value, as was wisely said of a niece of King [1] Gorboduc's. Know then that, if another than the coronet had received this script, he would not perchance have valued it so highly. The Sybil leaves had not so much consultation about them, nor were they half so chargeable as these are like to be. We have first sent them to Secretary Cook, imagining nothing but a state key could unlock those mysteries.

---

[1] [Old copy has, and perhaps Suckling wrote, *queene.*]

Now we are in quest of an Arabic figure-caster, for as much of it as we conceive is Chaldee or Syriac. The coronet believes there are noble things in it; but what Beaumont said of worth wrapped up in rivelled skin, he saith of this. Who would go in to fetch it out? Indeed the opinions about it have been different: some thought it a little against the state, others a ballad with the pictures the wrong way, and the most discreet have guessed it to be a collection of charms and spells, and have adventured to cut it into bracelets, to be distributed and worn by poor people as remedies against cramps and toothaches—only we will preserve the faces. And for Mistress Delaine's, we do not despair but Vandyke may be able to copy it. Threescore pounds we have offered, and I think fourscore will tempt him. For Mistress T[homas] there are in that certain *je ne sai quois*, which none but those that have studied it can discover, and Sir Anthony shall hold his hand till Mr H—— comes to town. This is all the favour can be done in this business by your humble servant,   J. S.

———

Sir,—Lest you think I had not as perfectly forgot you as you glory to have done me, let these lines assure you that, if at any time I think of you, it is with as much scorn as you vainly hitherto may have supposed it has been with affection; a certain general compassion in me, and pity of poor follies, of which number I take this to be one. A triumph, where there has been no conquest, has persuaded me to let you know this much.

And now, if that you have had so much faith as that you could believe a thing so impossible as that of my loving of you, would you but reduce yourself

to believe a thing so reasonable, as that there never was any such matter, you would make me step into a belief that you never yet had the good thoughts of
J. S.

[*To Aglaura (?)*]

THERE was (O seldom-happy word of *was !*) a time when I was not Montferrat ; and sure there was a time too, when all was handsome in my heart, for you were there, dear princess, and filled the place alone. *Were there* (O wretched word again !); and should you leave that lodging, more wretched than Montferrat needs must be your humble servant,
J. S.

To T[homas] C[arew].[1]

THOUGH writing be as tedious to me as no doubt reading will be to thee, yet considering that I shall drive that trade thou speakest of to the Indies, and for my beads and rattles have a return of gold and pearl, I am content for thy sake, and in private thus to do penance in a sheet.

Know then, dear Carew, that at eleven last night, flowing as much with love as thou hast ebbed, thy letter found me out. (I read, considered, and admired ;) and did conclude at last, that Horsley air did excel the waters of the Bath, just so much as love is a more noble disease than the pox.

---

[1] There is no collateral information extant, so far as we are aware, capable of throwing light on the allusions in this letter.

No wonder if the Countesses think time lost till they be there. Who would not be, where such cures flow? The care thou hast of me, that I should traffic right, draws me by way of gratitude to persuade thee to bottle us some of that, and send it hither to town. Thy returns will be quicker than those to the Indies; nor needst thou fear a vent, since the disease is epidemical.

One thing more: who knows, wouldst thou be curious in the search, but thou mayest find an air of contrary virtue about thy house, which may, as this destroys, so that create affection? If thou couldst,

> The lady of Highgate then should embrace
> The disease of the stomach and the word of disgrace.
> > Gredeline and grass-green
> > Shall sometimes be seen,
> > Its arms to entwine
> > About the woodbine.

In honest prose thus: we would carry ourselves first, and then our friends manage all the little loves at Court, make more Tower work, and be the Duke of B[uckingham] of our age, which without it we shall never be. Think on't, therefore, and be assured that, if thou joinest me in the patent with thee, in the height of all my greatness I will be thine, all but what belongs to Desdemona, which is just (as I mean) to venture at thy horse-race Saturday come seven-night.

J. S.

[*To a Lady respecting a Marriage.*]

It is none of the least discourtesies money hath done us mortals, the making things, easy in themselves and natural, difficult. Young and handsome people would have come together without half this trouble, if that had never been. This would tell you, madam, that the offer, having nothing about it of new, begot in our young lover very little of anything else but melancholy which, notwithstanding, I could easily perceive, grew rather from a fear of his father's mind, than a care of satisfying his own. That persuaded me to throw in all and add the last reserve, which fortunately turned the scale, the cavalier setting a greater rate, and truly, upon the kindness of it, than upon the thing, and in that showed the courtesy of his judgment, as well as his ability. The uncle is no less satisfied than the nephew, and both are confident to draw to the same thoughts, to whom (as it was fit) I have left the office.

And now, madam, you may safely conclude the cause to be removed out of Pluto's court into Cupid's —from the God of Moneys to the God of Love who, if he break not off old customers, will quickly despatch them, since he seldom delays those that have pass'd their trials in the other place.—Your humble servant,

J. S.

LETTER TO HENRY JERMYN.

[This is rather a short political essay than a letter, and, without partiality, may be pronounced a most remarkable State paper, considering the writer and the period of composition. It is in the highest degree creditable to Suckling's sagacity, foresight, and good sense, and shows, perhaps, as conclusively as possible, that he was much more than the mere "light and agreeable" author he has been represented.

The text here employed is the original one of 1641, where it forms a 4to. tract of eight leaves, with the title, of which we have given a representation below. It is, with certain changes and a few omissions, in all the editions of the "Fragmenta," where it is headed, " To Mr Henry German, in the beginning of Parliament, 1640." The text of 1641 has been corrected occasionally by those of 1646–48.

It is proper to explain that a design, which is still carried out as regards the matter in the Appendix, had been formed to reproduce all the separately-printed pieces by or relating to Suckling in their original shape, which may account for this exceptional departure from the rule of adopting modern orthography.]

A
COPPY
OF
A LETTER
FOVND IN THE
PRIVY LODGE-
INGS AT *WHITE-*
HALL.

Printed in the yeare,
1641.

A
COPPY OF A
LETTER FOVND
IN THE PRIVY LODG-
INGS AT *WHITE-*
HALL.

Hat it is fit for the King to doe fomething extraordinary at this prefent, is not onely the opinion of the wifeft, but their expectation alfo; men obferve him more now, then at other times : for Majefty in an eclipfe, like the Sunne, drawes eyes, that would not fo much as have looked towards it, if it had fhined out and appeared like it felfe. To lie ftill now, at leaft, fhewes but a calmeneffe of mind, not a magnanimitie : fince in matters of government to thinke well at any time (much more in a very active) is little better then to dreame well; nor muft hee ftay to act till his people defire, becaufe tis thought nothing relifheth with them leffe : for therefore hath nothing relifhed with them,

because

becaufe the King for the moft part hath ftayed till they
defired, and done nothing but what either they have,
or were peti[ti]oning for. But that the King fhould doe,
will not bee fo much the queftion, as what hee fhould
doe. And furely for the King to have right councell
given him at all times is ftrange, and at this time almoft impoffible ; his party for the moft part (I would
it were modeftly fpoken and it were not all of them)
have fo much to doe for their owne prefervation, that
they cannot, without breaking a law in nature, intend
anothers. Thofe that have courage, have not perchance
innocency, and fo dare not fhew themfelves in the
Kings bufineffe ; and if they have innocency, they want
parts to make themfelves confiderable, and fo confe-
quently the things they undertake. Then in the Court,
they give fuch councell as they beleeve the King is
inclined to, and determine of his good by his defire,
which is a kind of fetting the Sunne by the diall : intereft which cannot erre by paffion, which may. In going about to fhew the King a cure, a man fhould firft
fhew him the difeafe. But to Kings, as to fome kind
of patients, it is not alway proper to fhew them how ill
they are ; and is too much like a country clowne, not to
fhew the way unleffe hee know of you firft, from whence
you come, and difcourfe of things before. Kings may
bee miftaken, and Councellours corrupted, but true intereft alone (faid the Duke of *Rohan*) cannot erre. It
were not amiffe therefore to find out this intereft, for
fetting downe right principles before conclusions is
weighing the fcales before wee deale for the commodities.

Certainely the intereft of the King is the union of the
people, and whofoever hath told him otherwife, (as the
Scripture faith of the Divell) was a Seducer from the
first.

firſt. If there had beene one Prince in the whole
World, that made felicity in this life, and left a faire
fame after death, without the love of his Subjects, there
were some colour to defpife it. There was not among
all our princes a greater Courter of the people then
Richard the third; not fo much out of feare as out of
wifedome, and fhall the worſt of Kings have ſtriven for
that, and fhall not the beſt? it being an Angelicall
thing to gaine love.

There bee two things in which the people expect to
bee fatiffied, Religion and juſtice, nor can it bee done
by any little Acts, but by Reall and Kingly refolutions.
If any thinke that by dividing the factions (a good rule
at other times) hee fhall maſter the reſt, hee will bee
ftrangely deceived, for in beginning of things it would doe
much; but when whole Kingdomes are refolv'd. Of
thofe now that leade thofe parties, if you would take
off the major number the leffer would governe, and doe
the fame things ftill. Nay, if you could take off all,
they would fet up one and follow him; for as *Cato* faid
of the *Romans* they were like fheepe, and that the way
to drive them was in a flocke, for if one would bee extravagant, all the reſt would follow; fo it will bee here.
It will dearely appeare, that neither the perfon of the
Scottish or *English* Actours upon the ftage are confiderable to the great Body of *England*, but the things
they undertake, which, done by another hand and fo
done that there remaines no jealoufie, leaves them
where they were and not much rifen in value.[1] And of
how great confequence it is for the King to refume the

---

[1] [This passage is rather obscure; it is one of those omitted
in the " Fragmenta." Original has *and leaves*.]

right

right and bee Authour himfelfe, let any body judge; fince (as *Comines* faith) thofe that have the art to pleafe the people, have the power to raife them.

To doe things fo that there remaine no jealoufie is very neceffary, and is no more then really reforming, that is, pleafing them; for to doe things that fhall grieve hereafter, and yet pretend love, amongft Lovers themfelves, where there is the eafieft faith, will not bee accepted. It will not bee enough for the King to doe what they defire, but hee muft doe fomething more; for that will fhew the heartineffe; I meane by doing more, doing fomething of his owne, as throwing away things they call not for, or giving that they expected not; and when they fee the King doing the fame things with them, that will take away all thought or apprehenfion, that hee thinkes the things they have done already ill.

Now if the King ends the difference, and takes away the fufpect for the future, the caufe will fall out to bee no worfe, then when two dualifts enter the field, the worfted partie (the other having no ill opinion of him) hath his fword given him againe without any farther hurt, after hee hath beene in the others power. But otherwife it is not fafe to imagine what will follow, for the people are naturally not valiant, nor not much Cavalliers. Now tis the nature of Cowards to hurt when they receive none, and wound even the dead; they will not bee content, while they feare and have the upper hand, to fetter onely royaltie, but perchance, as timorous fpirits ufe, will not thinke themfelves fafe while it is at all. And poffibly this is now the ftate of things.

In this great worke, at leaft to make it appeare perfect and lafting to the Kingdome, it is neceffary that

the

the Queene really joyne : for if fhee ftand aloofe, there will bee ftill fufpition, it being a received opinion in the World, that fhee hath a great intereft in the Kings favour and power. And to invite her; fhee is to confider with her felfe, whether fuch great vertues and eminent excellencies (though fhee bee highly admired and valued by thofe that know her and are about her), ought to reft fatiffied with fo narrow a payment as the eftimation of a few, and whether it bee not more proper for a Queene fo great to aime at univerfall honour and love then private efteeme and value. Befides, how becoming a worke of the fweetneffe and foftneffe of her fex is compounding of differences and uniting hearts ; and how proper for a Queene, reconciling King and people!

There is but one thing more remaines, which whifperd abroad bufieth the Kings mind, if not difturbes it, in the midft of thefe great refolutions : and that is the prefervation of fome fervants, which hee thinkes fomewhat hardly torne from him of late, which is a thing of fo tender a nature, I fhall rather propound fomething about it then refolve it.

The firft Quere will bee, whether (as things now ftand) Kingdomes in the ballance, the King is not to follow nature, where the confervation of the generall weale commands and governes the leffe : as iron in particular fympathy fticks to the Load-ftone, but, if it be joyned with a greater body of Iron, it quits thofe particular affections to the Load-ftone, and moves with the other the greater body, the common Country.

The fecond will bee whether, if hee could preferve thefe Minifters, they can bee of any ufe to him hereafter, fince no man is ferved with a greater prejudice,
                                                              then

then hee that imployes fufpected Minifters, or not belov'd, though able and deferving in themfelves.

The third is, whether to preferve them there bee any other way then for the King firft to bee right with his people, fince the rule in Philofophy muft ever hold good : *nemo dat, quod non habet.* Before the King have power to preferve, hee muft have power.

And laftly, whether the way to preferve this power, bee not to give it away; for the people of *England* have ever bin like wantons, which pull and tugge as long as the Prince hath pulled with them, as you may fee in King *Henry* the third, King *Iohn*, and King *Edward* the fecond; and indeed all the troublefome and unfortunate raignes. But when the Princes have let it goe, the people come and put it in their hands againe, that they may play on, as you may see in Queene *Elizabeth.*

I will conclude all with a prayer, not that I thinke it needs for the prefent (prayers are to keepe us from what may bee, as well as preferve us from what is), that the King may not bee too unfenfible of what is without him, nor too refolv'd of what is within him. To bee ficke of a dangerous difeafe and feel no paine cannot bee but with loffe of underftanding : 'tis an Aphorifme of *Hippocrates.*

And on the other fide Opinioniftrie is
a fullen Porter, and (as is wit-
neffed of *Conftancy*) fhuts out
oftentimes better things
then it lets in.

FINIS.

AN ACCOUNT OF RELIGION.

An Account of Religion by Reason. A Discourse upon Occasion presented to the Earl of Dorset: By Sir John Suckling. Printed by his own Copy.

Lucret. page 227.   *Tentat enim dubiam mentem rationis egestas.*

A MS. copy of this essay is in the State Paper Office. John Lawson, the friend of Wordsworth, characterises Suck-ling's views on religion as "always just, sometimes profound." (MS. note in a copy of the "Fragmenta Aurea," 1658.)

I send you here, my lord, that discourse enlarged, which frighted the lady into a cold sweat, and which had like to have made me an atheist at court, and your lordship no very good Christian. I am not ignorant that the fear of Socinianism at this time renders every man that offers to give an account of religion by reason suspected to have none at all; yet I have made no scruple to run that hazard, not knowing why a man should not use the best weapon his Creator hath given him for his defence. That faith was by the apostles both highly exalted and severally enjoined, is known to every man, and this upon excellent grounds; for it was both the easiest and best way of converting, the other being tedious and almost useless, for but few among thousands are capable of it, and those few not capable at all times of their life, judgment being required. Yet the best servant our Saviour ever had upon earth was so far from neglecting or contemning reason, that his epistles were admired even by those that embraced not the truths he delivered; and, indeed, had the fathers of the Church only bid men believe, and not told them why, they had slept now unsainted in their graves, and as much benighted with oblivion as the ordinary parish priests of their own age.

That man is deceivable is true, but what part within him is not likelier than his reason? For as Manilius said—

Nam neque decipitur ratio nec decipit unquam.

And how unlikely is it that that which gives us the prerogative above other creatures, and wholly entitles us to future happiness, should be laid aside, and not used to the acquiring of it!

But by this time, my lord, you find how apt those which have nothing to do themselves are to give others trouble. I shall only therefore let you know that your commands to my Lord of Middlesex are performed; and that when you have fresh ones, you cannot place them where they will be more willingly received, than by your humble servant,

JOHN SUCKLING.

BATH, *Sept.* 2.

A Discourse of Religion.

———o———

AMONG the truths, my lord, which we receive, none more reasonably commands our belief than those which by all men at all times have been assented to. In this number, and highest, I place this great one—that there is a Deity, which the whole world had been so eager to embrace, that rather than it would have none at all, it hath too often been contented with a very mean one.

That there should be a great Disposer and Orderer of things, a wise Rewarder and Punisher of good and evil, hath appeared so equitable to men, that by instinct they have concluded it necessary. Nature, which doth nothing in vain, having so far imprinted it in us all that, should the envy of the predecessors deny the secret to succeeders, they yet would find it out. Of all those little ladders with which we scale heaven, and climb up to our Maker, that seems to me not the worst of which man is the first step. For but by examining how I, that could contribute nothing to mine own being, should be here, I come to ask the same question for my father, and so am led in a direct line to a last Producer, that must be more than man; for if man made man, why died not I when my father died? since, according to that maxim of the philosophers, the cause taken away, the effect does not remain. Or, if the first man gave himself being, why hath he it not still, since it were unreasonable to imagine anything could have power to give itself life, that had no power to continue it? That there is then a God, will not be so much the dispute as what this God is, or how to be worshipped—[this] is that which hath troubled poor mortals from the first; nor are they yet in quiet. So great has been the diversity, that some have almost thought God was no less delighted with variety in his service than he was pleased with it in his works. It would not be amiss to take a survey of the world from its cradle, and, with Varro, divide it into three ages—the Unknown, the Fabulous, and the Historical.

The first was a black night, and discovered nothing; the second was a weak and glimmering light, representing things imperfectly and falsely; the last, more clear, left handsome monuments to posterity. The unknown I place in the age before the Flood, for that deluge swept away things as well as men, and left not so much as footsteps to trace them by. The fabulous began after the Flood; in this time godheads were cheap, and men, not knowing where to choose better, made deities one of another. Where this ended, the historical took beginning; for men began to engrave in pillars, and to commit to letters, as it were by joint-consent; for the three great epochs or terms of accompt were all established within the space of thirty years, the Grecians reckoning from their Olympiads, the Romans from the building of their city, and the Babylonians from their King Psalmanasar. To bring into the scale with Christian religion anything out of the first age we cannot, because we know nothing of it.

And the second was so fabulous, that those which took it up afterwards smiled at it as ridiculous and false, which, though, was easier for them to do than to show a true. In the historical it improved and grew more refined ; but here the fathers entered the field, and so clearly gained the victory, that I should say nothing in it, did I not know it still to be the opinion of good wits that the particular religion of Christians has added little to the general religion of the world. Let us take it, then, in its perfect estate, and look upon it in that age, which was made glorious by the bringing forth of so many admirable spirits. And this was about the eightieth Olympiad, in the year of the world 3480 ; for in the space of 100 years flourished almost all that Greece could boast of—Socrates, Plato, Aristotle, Architas, Isocrates, Pythagoras, Epicurus, Heraclitus, Zenophon, Zeno, Anaxagoras, Democritus, Demosthenes, Parmenides, Zenocrates, Theophrastus, Empedocles, Tymæus, with divers others, orators and poets. Or rather (for they had their religion one from another, and not much different), let us take a view of it in that century in which Nature, as it were to oppose the Grecian insolence, brought forth that happy birth of Roman wits—Varro, Cicero, Cæsar, Livy, Sallust, Virgil, Horace, Vitruvius, Ovid, Pliny, Cato, Marcus Brutus ; and this was from Quintus Servilius his consulship to that of Augustus, 270 years after the other. And to say truth, a great part of our religion, either directly or indirectly, hath been professed by heathens, which I conceive not so much an exprobation to it as a confirmation, it being no derogating from truth to be warranted by common consent.

First, then, the creation of the world is delivered almost the same in the Phœnician stories with that in Moses ; from this the Grecians had their chaos, and Ovid the beginning of his " Metamorphosis." That all things were made by God was held by Plato and others; that darkness was before light, by Thales; that the stars were made by God, by Aratus; that life was infused into things by the breath of God, Virgil; that man was made of dust, Hesiod and Homer; that the first life of man was in simplicity and nakedness, the Egyptians taught; and from thence the poets had their golden age. That in the first times men's lives lasted a thousand years, Berosus and others; that something divine was seen amongst men till that the greatness of our sins gave them cause to remove, Catullus; and this he that writes the story of Columbus reports from the Indians; of a great deluge, almost all. But to the main they hold one God; and though multiplicity hath been laid to their charge, yet certainly the clearer spirits understood these petty gods as things, not as deities : second causes and several virtues of the great power —by Neptune, water; Juno, air; by Dispater, earth; by Vulcan, fire. And sometimes one god signified many things, as Jupiter the whole world, the whole heaven; and sometimes many gods one thing, as Ceres, Juno Magna, the earth. They concluded those to be vices which we do; nor was there much difference in their virtues, only Christians have made ready belief the highest, which they would hardly allow to be any. They held rewards for the good and punishments for the ill; had their Elysium and their hell; and that they thought the pains eternal there is evident in that they believed from thence was no return. They proportioned sufferings hereafter to offences here; as in Tantalus, Sisyphus, and others, among which that of conscience, the worm that never dies, was one, as in the vulture's gnawing of Prometheus's heart, and Virgil's ugliest of furies thundering in Pirithous' ear, was not obscurely shown; and (yet nearer us) they held the number of the elect to be but small, and that there should be a last day, in which the world should perish by fire. Lastly, they had their priests, temples, altars.

We have seen now the parallel; let us inquire whether those things they seem to have in common with us, we have not in a more excellent manner; and whether the rest, in which we differ from all the world, we take not up with reason. To begin, then, with their Jupiter (for all before were but little stealths from Moses' works)—how much more like a deity are the actions our stories declare our God to have done, than what the ethnic authors deliver of theirs? How excellently elevated are our descriptions of Him, theirs looking as if they knew that power only by their fears, as their statutes erected to him declare, for when he was Capitolinus, he appeared with thunder; when Latiaris, besmeared with blood; when Feretrius, yet more terrible. We may guess what their conceptions were by the worship they gave him. How full of cruelty were their sacrifices, it being received almost through the whole world that gods were pleased with the blood of men; and this custom neither the Grecian wisdom nor Roman civility abolished, as appears by [the] sacrifices to Bacchus.

Then the ceremonies of Liber Pater and Ceres, how obscene! and those days, set apart for the honour of the gods, celebrated with such shows as Cato himself was ashamed to be present at. On the contrary, our services are such as not only Cato, but God himself, may be there. We worship Him, that is the purest Spirit, in purity of spirit; and did we not believe what the Scriptures deliver from Himself, yet would our reason persuade us that such an essence could not be pleased with the blood of beasts, or delighted with the steam of fat; and in this particular Christians have gone beyond all others except the Mahometans, besides whom there has been no nation that had not sacrifice, and was not guilty of this pious cruelty.

That we have the same virtues with them is very true; but who can deny that those virtues have received additions from Christianity, conducing to men's better living together? Revenge of injuries Moses both took himself and allowed by the law to others; Cicero and Aristotle placed it in virtue's quarter. We extol patient bearing of injuries; and what quiet the one, what trouble the other, would give the world, let the indifferent judge. Their justice only took care that men should not do wrong; ours, that they should not think it, the very coveting severely forbidden; and this holds, too, in chastity: desire of a woman unlawfully being as much a breach of the commandment as the enjoying, which showed not only the Christian's care, but wisdom to prevent ill, who provided to destroy it, where it was weakest, in the cradle, and declared He was no less than a God which gave them these laws; for had He been but man, He never would have provided or taken care for what He could not look into, the hearts of men, and what He could not punish, their thoughts. What charity can be produced answerable to that of Christians? Look upon the primitive times, and you shall find that, as if the whole world had been but a private family, they sent from province to province, and from places far distant, to relieve them they never saw nor knew.

Now for the happiness which they proposed. If they take it as the heathens understood it, it was an Elysium, a place of blessed shades, at best but a handsome retirement from the troubles of this world; if according to the duller Jews, feastings and banquetings (for it is evident that the Sadducees, who were great observers of the Mosaical law, had but faint thoughts of anything to come) there being in Moses'

books no promises but of temporal blessings, and if
any, an obscure mention of eternity. The Mahometans are no less sensual, making the renewing
of youth, high feasts, a woman with great eyes, and
dressed up with a little more fancy, the last and best
good.

Then the hell. How gentle with the heathens—
but the rolling of a stone, filling of a sieve with water,
sitting before banquets and not daring to touch them,
exercising the trade and businesses they had on
earth. With the Mahometans, but a purgatory acted
in the grave, some pains inflicted by a bad angel,
and those qualified and mitigated too by an assisting
good one. Now, for the Jews, as they had no hopes,
so they had no fears. If we consider it rightly,
neither their punishments were great enough to deter
them from doing ill, nor their rewards high enough
to invite men to strictness of life; for, since every
man is able to make as good a heaven of his own, it
were unreasonable to persuade him to quit that certain happiness for an uncertainty; whereas Christians, with as much more noble consideration both
in their heaven and hell, took care not only for the
body but the soul, and for both above man's appre-
hension.

The strangest, though most epidemical, disease of
all religions has been an imagination men have had
that the imposing painful and difficult things upon
themselves was the best way to appease the Deity,
grossly thinking the chief service and delight of the
Creator to consist in the tortures and sufferings of
the creature. How laden with chargeable and un-
necessary ceremonies the Jews were, their feasts,
circumcisions, sacrifices, great Sabbaths and little
Sabbaths, fasts, burials, indeed almost all their worship, sufficiently declare; and that the Mahometans
are much more infected appears by the cutting of

the prepuce, wearing iron rings in the skin of their foreparts, lancing themselves with knives, putting out their eyes upon the sight of their prophet's tomb, and the like. Of these last we can show no patterns amongst us; for though there be such a thing as whipping of the body, yet it is but in some parts of Christendom, and there perchance too more smiled at than practised. Our religion teaches us to bear afflictions patiently when they fall upon us, but not to force them upon ourselves; for we believe the God we serve wise enough to choose His own service, and therefore presume not to add to His commands. With the Jews, it is true, we have something in common, but rather the names than things, our fasts being more the medicines of the body than the punishments of it: spiritual as our Sabbaths: both good men's delight, not their trouble.

But, lest this discourse should swell into a greatness such as would make it look rather like a defence, which I have laboured to get, than an accompt which I always carry about me, I will now briefly examine whether we believe not with reason those things we have different from the rest of the world. First, then, for the persuasion of the truth of them in general, let us consider what they were that conveyed them to us men, of all the world, the most unlikely to plot the cosenage of others, being themselves but simple people, without ends, without designs: seeking neither honour, riches, nor pleasure, but suffering, under the contrary, ignominy, poverty, and misery: enduring death itself, nay, courting it; all which are things distasteful to nature, and such as none but men strangely assured would have undergone. Had they feigned a story, certainly they would not in it have registered their own faults, nor delivered Him, whom they propounded as a God, ignominiously crucified. Add to this the progress their doctrine

made abroad, miraculous above all other, either
before or since; other religions were brought in with
the sword, power forcing a custom, which by degrees
usurped the place of truth, in this even power itself
opposing; for the Romans, contrary to their custom,
which entertained all religions kindly, persecuted
this, which by its own strength so possessed the
hearts of men that no age, sex, or condition refused
to lay down life for it.   A thing so rare in other
religions that, among the heathens, Socrates was the
sole martyr; and the Jews (unless of some few under
Manasses and Antiochus) have not to boast of any.
If we cast our eyes upon the healing of the blind,
curing the lame, redeeming from the grave, and but
with a touch or word we must conclude them done
by more than humane power, and if by any other, by
no ill: these busy not themselves so much about the
good of man.   And this religion not only forbids by
precept the worship of wicked spirits, but in fact destroys it, wheresoever it comes.   Now, as it is clear
by authors impartial (as being no Christians) that
strange things were done, so it is plain they were done
without imposture.   Delusions shun the light; these
were all acted openly, the very enemies both of the
Master and disciples daily looking on.   But let us
descend to those more principal particulars which so
much trouble the curious wits—these I take to be the
Incarnation, Passion, Resurrection, and Trinity.

For the first. That man should be made without
man, why should we wonder more at it, in that time
of the world, than in the beginning? Much easier,
certainly, it was here, because nearer the natural way
—woman being a more prepared matter than earth.
Those great truths and mysteries of salvation would
never have been received without miracles; and
where could they more opportunely be shown than
at His entrance into the world, where they might

give credit to His following actions and doctrine?
So far it is from being against my reason to think
Him thus born, that it would be against it to believe
Him otherwise, it being not fit that the Son of God
should be produced like the race of men. That
humane nature may be assumed by a Deity, the
enemy of Christians, Julian, confirms, and instances
(himself) in Æsculapius, whom he will have descend
from heaven in mortal shape, to teach us here below
the art of physic. Lastly, that God has lived with
men, has been the general fancy of all nations, every
particular having this tradition, that the Deity at
some time or other conversed amongst men. Nor is
it contrary to reason to believe Him residing in glory
above, and yet incarnate here. So, in man himself,
the soul is in heaven when it remains in the flesh,
for it reacheth with its eye the sun. Why may not
God then, being in heaven, be at the same time with
us in the flesh, since the soul without the body
would be able to do much more than with it, and God
much more than the soul, being the soul of the soul?
But it may be urged as more abstruse, how all in
heaven, and all in earth? Observe man speaking (as
you have done seeing); is not the same speech, at
the instant it is uttered, all in every place? receives
not each particular ear alike the whole, and shall not
God be much more ubiquitary than the voice of man?
For the Passion (to let alone the necessity of satisfying divine justice this way which, whosoever reads
more particularly our divines, shall find rationally
enforced), we find the heathen had something near
to this, though, as in the rest, imperfect, for they
sacrificed single men for the sins of the whole city or
country. Porphyrius, having laid this foundation,
that the supreme happiness of the soul is to see God,
and that it cannot see Him unpurified, concludes
that there must be a way for the cleansing of man-

kind ; and proceeding to find it out, he tells that arts and sciences serve but to set our wits right in the knowledge of things, and cleanse us not enough to come to God. The like judgment he gives of purging by theurgy, and by the mysteries of the sun ; because those things extend but to some few, whereas this cleansing ought to be universal for the benefit of all mankind—in the. end resolves, that this cannot be done but by one of the three In-beginnings, which is the word they use to express the Trinity by. Let us see what the divinest of the heathens, and his master Plato, delivers to admiration, and as it were pro- phetically, to this purpose. "That a truly just man be shown," saith he, "it is necessary that he be spoiled of his ornaments, so that he must be accounted by others a wicked man, be scoffed at, put in prison, beaten, nay, be crucified ; " and certainly for Him that was to appear the highest example of patience, it was necessary to undergo the highest trial of it, which was an undeserved death.

Concerning the Resurrection, I conceive the diffi- culty to lie not so much upon our Lord as us—it being with easy reason imagined, that He which can make a body can lay it down and take it up again. There is something more that urges and presses us ; for [if] in our estate we promise ourselves hereafter, there will be no need of food, copulation, or excre- ment, to what purpose should we have a mouth, belly, or less comely parts? it being strange to imagine God to have created man for a moment of time, a body consisting of particulars which should be useless to all eternity. Besides, why should we desire to carry that along with us which we are ashamed of here, and which we find so great a trouble, that very wise men, were it not forbidden, would throw it off, before it were worn out? To this I should answer that, as the body is partner in well or ill doing, so it is but just it should share in the rewards or punishments hereafter; and though by reason of sin we blush at it here, yet when that shall cease to be, why we should be more ashamed than our first parents were, or some in the last-discovered parts of the world are now, I cannot understand. Who knows but these unsightly parts shall remain for good use, and that, putting us in mind of our imperfect estate here, they shall serve to increase our content and happiness there? What kind of thing a glorified body shall be, how changed, how refined, who knows? Nor is it the meanest invitement to me now to think that my estate there is above my capacity here. There remains that which does not only quarrel with the likelihood of a resurrection, but with the possibility; alleging that man, corrupted into dust, is scattered almost into infinity, or devoured by an irrational creature: goes into aliment, and grows part of it; then that creature, perchance, is made like food to another; and truly did we doubt God's power, or not think Him omnipotent, this were a labyrinth we should be lost in. But it were hard, when we see every petty chemic in his little shop bring into one body things of the same kind, though scattered and disordered, that we should not allow the great Maker of all things to do the same in His own University.

There remains only the mystery of the Trinity, to the difficulty of which the poverty and narrowness of words have made no small addition.

St Austin plainly says the word person was taken up by the Church for want of a better. Nature, substance, essence, hypostasis, suppositum, and persona have caused sharp disputes amongst the doctors; at length they are contented to let the three first and three last signify the same thing. By all of them is understood something complete, perfect, and singular; in this only they differ, that nature, substance, essence, are communicable *ad quid* and *ut quo*, as they call it; the other are not at all. But enough of this. Those that were the immediate conveyers of it to us wrapt it not up in any of these terms. We then hold God to be one and but one, it being gross to imagine two Omnipotents, for then neither would be so; yet since this good is perfectly good, and perfect goodness cannot be without perfect love, nor perfect love without communication (nor to an unequal or created, for then it must be inordinate); we conclude a Second Coeternal, though Begotten; nor are these contrary, though they seem to be so, even in created substances, that one thing may come from another, and yet that, from whence it comes, not be before that which comes from it, as in the sun and light. But in these high mysteries similitudes may be the best arguments. In metaphysics, they tell us, that to the constituting of every being there is a *posse sui esse*, from whence there is a *sapientia sui esse;* and from these two proceedeth an *amor sui esse:* and though these three be distinct, yet they may make up one perfect being. Again, and more familiarly, there is an hidden original of waters in the earth; from this a spring flows up; and of these proceeds a stream. This is but one essence, which knows neither a before nor an after, but in order—and that, too, according to our considering of it—the head of a spring is not a head but in respect of the spring; for if something flowed not from it, it were no original; nor the spring a spring, if it did not flow from something; nor the stream a stream but in respect of both. Now, all these three are but one water, and though one is not the other, yet they can hardly be considered one without the other. Now, though I know this is so far from a demonstration, that it is but an imperfect instance (perfect being impossible, of infinite by finite things), yet there is a resemblance great enough to let us see the possibility.

And here the eye of reason needed no more the spectacles of faith, than for these things of which we make sympathy the cause, as in the loadstone, or antipathy, of which every man almost gives instance from his own nature ; nor is it here so great a wonder that we should be ignorant ; for this is distant and removed from sense, these near and subject to it ; and it were stranger for me to conclude that God did not work *ad extra*, thus one and distinct, within Himself, because I cannot conceive how begotten, how proceeding ; than if a clown should say the hand of a watch did not move because he could not give an account of the wheels within. So far is it from being unreasonable, because I do not understand it, that it would be unreasonable I should. For why should a created substance comprehend an uncreated —a circumscribed and limited, an uncircumscribed and unlimited? And this I observe in those great lovers and lords of reason, quoted by the fathers, Zoroastes, Trismegistus, Plato, Numenius, Plotinus, Proclus, Amelius, and Avicen, that when they spoke of this mystery of the Trinity, of which all writ something, and some almost as plainly as Christians themselves, that they discussed it not as they did other things, but delivered them, as oracles which they had received themselves, without dispute.

Thus much of Christian profession compared with others. I should now show which, compared within itself, ought to be preferred ; but this is the work of every pen, perhaps to the prejudice of religion itself. This excuse, though, it has, that (like the chief empire), having nothing to conquer, no other religion to oppose or dispute against, it hath been forced to admit of civil wars, and suffer under its own excellency.

APPENDIX.

A
LETTER SENT
BY
SIR IOHN SVCK-
LING FROM

France, deploring his fad
Eftate and flight:
VVith a difcoverie of the plot
and confpiracie, intended
By him and his adherents
againft England.

Imprinted at London. 1641.

A Letter fent by Sir *John Suck-ling* from *France*, deploring his
fad Eftate and flight :
With a difcoverie of the plot
and confpiracie, intended by
him and his adherents
againft *England*.

1 Goe, dolefull fheet to everie ftreet
  Of London round about-a,
And tell'um all thy mafters fall
That lived bravely mought-a,

  2 Sir John in fight as a brave wight,
As the Knight of the Sun-a,
  Is forc'd to goe away with woe,
And from his countrie run-a,

  3 Vnhappy ftars to breed fuch iars,
That England's chief *Suckling*-a,
  Should prove of late the fcorn of fate
And fortunes unlucklin-a,

  4 But ye may fee inconftancie
In all things under heaven-a:
  When God withdraws his gracious laws
We run at fixe and feven-a,

5 Alas.

5 Alas, alas, how things doe paſſe :
What bootes a handſome face-a,
  A pretty wit and leggs to it
Not ſeaſond well with grace-a ?

  6 I that in court have made ſuch ſport
As never yet was found-a,
  And tickled all both great and ſmall
The Maides of honour round-a

  7 I that did play both night and day
And revelled here and there-a,
  Had change of ſuits, made layes to lutes
And bluſter'd everie where-a :

  8 I that could write and well indite
As 'tis to Ladies known-a,
  And bore the praiſe for ſongs and playes
Far more then were mine own-a,

  9 I that did lend and yearly ſpend
Thouſands out of my purſe-a,
  And gave the King a wondrous thing,
at once a hundred horſe-a.

  10 Bleſt providence that kept my ſence
So well, that I fond elſe-a,
  Should chance to hit to have the wit,
To keep one for my ſelfe-a

  11 I that marcht forth into the *North*,
And went up hills a main-a
  With ſword and lance like king of France,
And ſo came down againe-a.

  12 I that have done ſuch things, the Sun
And moone did never ſee-a,
  Yet now poore John, a pox upon
The fates, is faine to flee-a.

13 And for the brave, I uf'd to have
In all I wore or eate-a
　Accurffed chance to fpoyle the dance,
I fcarce have clothes or meate-a

14 Could not the plot, By which I got
Such credit in the play-a
　Aglaura bright that Perfian wight,
My roving fancie ftay-a,

15 But I muft flie at things fo high,
Above me not allow'd-a?
　And I Sir John, like Ixion,
For Juno kiffe a cloud-a?

16 Would I had burn'd it, when I turn'd it
Out of a Comedie-a:
　There was an omen in the nomen
(I feare) of Tragedie-a,

17 Which is at laft upon me caft
And I proclaim'd a fott-a
　For thinking to with Englifh doe
As with a Perfian plot-a

18 But now I finde with griefe of minde
What will not me availe-a,
　That plots in ieft are ever beft,
When plots in earneft faile-a.

19 Why could not I in time efpie
My errour; but whats worfe-a,
　Vnhappy vermin muft bring in *Iermin*
The mafter of the horfe-a

20 The valiant *Percie* God have mercie
Vpon his noble foule-a;
　Though hee be wife by my advice
Was in the plot moft foule-a

21 The wittie poet (Let all known it)
Davenant by name-a,
   In this defigne, that I call mine,
I utterlie difclaime-a

22 Though he can write, he cannot fight,
And bravely take a fort-a :
   Nor can he fmell a proiect well,
His nofe it is to[o] fhort-a

23 Tis true wee met, in counfell fet,
And plotted here in profe-a,
   And what he wanted, it is granted,
A bridge made of his nofe-a,

24 But to impart it to his art,
Wee had made prittie ftuffe-a.
   No, for the plot, that we had got,
One poet was enough-a.

25 Which had not fate and prying ftate
Crufht in the very wombe-a,
   We had ere long by power ftrong
Made England but one tombe-a.

26 Oh what a fright had bred that fight,
When Ireland, Scotland, France-a,
   Within the wall of London all
In feverall troopes fhould prance-a.

27 When men quarter'd, women flaughter'd
In heapes everie where-a,
   So thick fhould lie, the enemie
The very fight fhould fcare-a.

28 That they afraid of what they made,
A ftreame of blood fo high-a,

For fafety fled Should mount the dead
And unto heaven get nigh-a.

29 The fcarlet gowne and belt i'th towne
Each other would bewaile-a
 That their fhut purfe had brought this curfe,
That did fo much prevaile-a.

30 Each *Alderman* in his own chaine,
Being hang'd up like a dog-a,
 And all the city without pitty,
Made but one bloody bog-a.

31 The Irifh Kerne in battell fterne
For all their faults fo foul-a :
 Pride, ufe, ill gaine, and want of braine,
Teaching them how to howle-a.

32 No longer then the fine women
The Scots would praife and truft-a :
 The wanton Dames being burnt in flames
Far hotter then their luft-a.

33 But too too late lament their fate,
And miferie deplore-a
 By the French knocks having got a pox,
Worfe than they had before-a.

34 Infants unborne fhould fcape the horne
By being murther'd then-a ;
 Which they were fure if life indure
To have when they were men-a.

35 The precife frie, that now mounts high,
Full lowe we caft their Lot-a,
 And all that thinke it fin to drinke,
We doom'd unto the pot-a.

36 The

36 The Parliament is fully bent
To roote up Bifhops cleane-a,
  To raze their fort and fpoile their fport
We did intend and meane-a.

37 With many things confufion bringes
To Kingdoms in an hour-a,
  To burne up tillage, fack and pillage,
And handfome maides deflour-a.

38 But Argus eye did foon efpy
What we fo much did truft-a.
  And to our fhame and loffe of fame
Our plot laid in the duft-a.

39 And had we ftaid, I am affraid
That their *Briarian* hand-a
  Had ftruck us dead (who now are fled)
And ceifed all our land-a.

40 But thanks to heaven, three of the feven,
That were the plotters chiefe-a,
  Have led to France their wits a dance
To finde out a reliefe-a.

41 But *Davenant* fhakes and Buttons makes
As ftrongly with his breech-a.
  As hee ere long did with his tongue
Make many a bombaft fpeech-a.

42 But yet we hope hee'le fcape the rope,
That now him fo doth fright-a :
  The Parliament being content
That he this fact fhould write-a.

From Paris, Iune 16, 1641.

Finis.   *I. S. K.*

Four fugitives meeting

OR,

The Difcourfe amongft my *Lord Finch*,
Sir *Francis Windebank*, Sir

Iohn Sucklin, and

Doctor Roane, as they accidentally met

in *France*, with a detection of

their feverall pranks in

ENGLAND.

Printed In the Yeare, 1641.

[The original tract has on the title page a common ballad cut, not in any way belonging to it; and it did not therefore seem worth while to have it copied.]

Foure Fugitives meeting, &c.

Suckling.

IMmenſe Doctor *Roan*, you are moſt happily encountred, they have wiſht your Company a long time in England, the poor Civilians look like ſpirits now they are deprived of their body.

Roan. Body, Sir John, what doe you meane?

Suck. Why, the Body of the civill Law, *Corpus Iuris Civilis,* for ſo they call you.

Roan. And pardon of your Poetry, how fare your hundred Horſe i' th North, doe they ſtand to their colours, now their Commander is fled? I wonder much, Sir John, that you being a noble Gentleman, a Commander, and a Volunteere, that [you] would leave your poore ſouldiers without pay, and come away without taking leave of your Friends.

Wind. I heard that Sir John had made a new play and for feare leſt it ſhould be hiſt off the ſtage, betooke himſelfe to travell.

Finch. And I have heard, that by reaſon of his absence

abfence, that play was not worth the ftudying, there was an intricate plot in it that could not well be underftood, there were two Poets in it that were found to bee the chiefe Politicians, which the State perceiving, made diligent pursuit after them, the one whereof had the happineffe to efcape, the other was apprehended, and then the Play ended, before the Poets execution : which was very much difliked.

Suck. How came you to the knowledge of this, my good Lord Finch? you doe not flye over into England every night, and there load your felfe with newes againft the morning, doe you?

Wind. No, Sir John, he needes not, wee were informed by———

Suck. Spare your Wind, good M. Secretary Windebank, I perceive you hold intelligence with those Jefuits, you compounded withall at fo eafie a rate.

Roan. Still you are befide the marke; we were inform'd, Sir John, by one *Kilfcot,* one of your Worfhips Cap and Feather men, who came over hither to know if your voyage into *Portugal* held or no; he faid that fome two or three hundred buffe-men did much admire, that now the way is faire, you will not be their guide; they would fane have kift their difcontented Colonels hand before he miftooke *France* for *Portugall;* but you were fo unkind to leave them on a fudden.

Hold

Suc. Hold there, good Doctor *Roane,* and take me
with you : you are to be blam'd too, for not bidding
farewell to Sir *Paul Pinder,* (at whofe beauteous
houfe you have devoured the carkaſſe of many a
cram'd Capon) before you fled : but I wonder more,
why you came hither fo unprovided; methinks fome
Englifh dyet would have bin good for a weake
ftomack : the Church-Wardens of North-hampton-
ſhire promifed to give you a good fee, if you will goe
to 'em, and refolve 'em whether they may lawfully
take the oath &c. or no.

Wind. That may very well be, for they have given
him a great Addition : they ftile him Og the great
Commiſſary, they fay he was as briske in difcharging
the new Canons, as he that made them ; but I pray, Sir
John, relate the caufe of your comming hither.

Suc. Then muft I addreſſe my felfe to you, my
good Lord Finch ; I have fome papers to deliver you
from the commons of England, who are forry they are
deprived your company, and promife if your Lord-
ſhip will go into England and collect the ship money,
they will with all willingneſſe pay you.

Finch. With a Powder will they not, Sir John ? you
have not forgot the skirmiſh i'th North, have you ? you
call the poore Scots Pedlars, but they were angry, and
made your fiery horfe run away with you.

Wind. I thinke, Sir John, your coat of Male would
fcarce

fcarce have kept out the Pedlars bullets, as it did the Rapier in Black-fryars, when you came from *Aglauro*.

Suc. No more, I believe, would your high and mighty ftate have fecured your neck, had you ftaid there.

Wind. I am of opinion, that my Lord of *Canterbury* would remit the greateft fine in the high Commiffion, on the condition hee were here; but I believe, if I had ftaid, all his Tobacco would not have cur'd the ftopping in my throat; if it fecure his owne, tis well.

Suc. For my part, I ever held my head to be my felfe, and honour to be but my neighbour; and the rules of nature command me to love my felfe better then my neighbour. I lov'd honour well, but not with fuch a zeale to venture my life for her, when I my felfe could never enjoy her.

Roan. Well faid of all fides! why fhould we that are all alike, fall out? come, lets to dinner, you fhall fall to your dainty difhes, but give me a rib and a leg, Roaft-beefe and Capon, the very meat I eate at the commons, and then after dinner wee'l play a game at Ticktake or Irish for halfe a pounde of reafons.

Suc. Pox upon reafons! I cannot endure your
mechanicke

mechanicke games. Ile play at Inne and Inne for a Piece the Caſter—my old game.

Wind. No, Sir John, you may excuſe your friends, and uſe the art of ſtirring a dye to ſtrangers : win their money and welcome.

Finch. I, Sir John, 'tis charity to cheat the Mon-ſieurs, you uſe your Quick-ſilverd dye amongſt them as ſecurely as you could in England, and when you have got their money, wee'l ſpend it bravely.

Suc. Come, my brave boyes, money weel never lack,
But drowne our ſorrowes in a cup of Sack.

FINIS.

NEWES

FROM SIR

JOHN SVCKLIN

BEING

A RELATION

OF HIS

CONVERSION

FROM

A PAPIST TO A PROTESTANT.

Alſo,

What Torments he endured by thoſe of the *Inquiſition* in
SPAINE,

And how the Lord Lekeux his Accuſer, was ſtrucken dumbe,
hee going to have the Sentence of Death paſſe upon him.

Sent in a Letter to the Lord Conway, *now being in Ireland.*

Printed for M. Rookes, *and are to be ſold in Grubſtreet,* 1641.

N E W E S

FROM

Sir John Sucklin.

T is an old proverb that he far
runs, that never turns; as will be
now made apparent by this enfuing
ftory, which will treat of one which
was accounted a treacherous and
disloyall Subject, and not long
fince made an efcape out of this
Kingdome, by name Sir *John* Suclin, who was fup-
pofed to be a *Romanift*, but now will his fufferings
make manifeft to the contrary.

When firft he flew out of this Kingdome, he took
up his habitation in *Roan*, belonging to the King of
France: but there fome difcontent growing between
another Knight [and] himfelfe, he left Roan, and to
Paris he bent his journey, where he had much honour
attributed

attributed to him, in refpect of his furnifhing a hundred men and horfes againft the *Scots*, in the time of Diffention between both Kingdomes.

In *Paris* as aforefaid, he lived in great honor, where he fell in league with the Lady *Damaife*, nigh kinfwoman to the Dutcheff of *Sheverey*, but a proteftant.

This Lady bore affection to him, after the fame manner that he did to her, but upon this condition, that he fhould purge himfelfe of all popifh dregs whatfoever.

To which hee moft willingly condifcended, and thereupon renounced the Pope with all his Complices.

But this is requifit to be declared, that there was a Lord in *Paris*, by name *Lequeux*, which bore affection to the fame Lady, and, to have his defire, invented a plot to take away Sir *John Sucklins* life; but he, having notice thereof, acquainted his lady with the pretended purpofe of the Lord *Lequeux*, whereupon fhe defired him to flye to fome other parts.

But his reply was, enjoying her fociety hee would be ambitious to flye any whither, but otherwife to flay; the worft thing which could happen, would be but death, and not to enjoy her company would be no leffe.

To whofe requeft fhe willingly granted; and in a fhort fpace they together tooke fhipping, and fayled to the hither parts of Spaine, whereas thefe two Turtles without any interception thought for to be.

But, alas! Fortune did prove adverfe againft them, and inftead of bleffing their hope with a profperous

Gale,

Gale, fhe played the part of ftorming Boreas, and fplit their fhip againft an envious Rocke.

For being arrived fafely, as they did thinke, within the Confines of Spaine, the afore-named malicious Lord *Lequeux*, having notice given of their efcape, prefently purfued them, and having overtaken them, complained to the great Arch-prieft of Spaine, how that they were both Traytors to *Rome*, and were arrived in *Spaine* for no other caufe, but to confpire the death of the great Mafter, and King of Spaine.

To confirme and bind which accufation, he fwore by the Sacrament, and facred body of Chrift.

Whereupon the *Arch-prieft* committed Sir *John Suclin* to the cuftody of thofe of the *Inquifition*, and his Lady to a clofe prifon, command being given that, unleffe Sir *John Suclin* did recant from any intent to doe injury unto the Church of *Rome*, that he fhould not want for torments, according to the antient cuftom of the *Inquifition*. Sir *John* made answer thus : That both his Lady and himfelfe were accufed falfely ; for although he bore no affection to the church of *Rome*, yet was he far from any intent for doing the leaft Member of it any wrong : much more the King of *Spaine* himfelfe, chiefe Agent to the *Pope*.

Notwithftanding, hee was committed, and fuffered thofe torments which are commonly inflicted upon thofe which are prifoners to the *Inquifition*. Once had he the *Spanifh Strapado;* twice tortured by fharpe needles, three times did he lodge in a ftinking Dungeon, and upon the fourth day was carryed to heare the Sentence of Death paffe upon him ; but was

miraculoufly

miraculoufly delivered; for the Lord *Lequex*, going
to accufe him the fecond time, was ftruck downe, and
by fignes firft, and then by writing, did confeffe to the
whole Affembly, that hee had falfely accufed Sir John
Suclin and his Lady.

Whereupon they were both delivered, and the Lord
Lequex committed to tortures.

Sir John and his Lady are now living
at the *Hague in Holland*, pioufly
and religioufly, and grieves
at nothing, but that
he did the King-
dome of Eng-
land wrong.

× ×
×

FINIS.

AN
ELEGIE
VPON THE
DEATH
OF THE
RENOWNED
SIR
IOHN SVTLIN.

Printed in the Yeare, 1642.

ELEGY VPON

Death of the Renowned

Sᴿ IOHN SVTLIN.

I had thought (great King of Poets) thy death muſt
Have raiſ'd the meaneſt ſtationer from the duſt ;
Inſpir'd with ſacred raptures every pen
Dead *Sutlin* living in the mouths of men ;
That from thy[1] confum'd Pile there would have
  flowne,
Amazing us, more Phœnixes then one.
All Preſſes would have groan'd, and Preſſe-men too
Swear at the thought, how much they had to doe.
Pardon me, Reader, if that I did think,
The very drops would have waſh'd away the Inke :
As when warm'd *Vulcan* to make armes was wonne,
Not for his owne, but for the faire Venus, sonne.

Such

---

[1] [Original *they*.]

Such was his ardent and inflam'd defire,
The fweaty ftreames had almoft quenfht the fire.
Naught feen in every towne but watry eyes,
And no booke read but *Sutlins* Elegies.
What, not one line, one word, one teare, not any :
To fing him dead, who hath eternizd many ?
What is become of *Davenant*, who alone,
And onely he, is able to bemone
So great a loffe ? Thou too maift praife his wit
With all the fkill thou haft, not equall it :
Speake, learned Davenant, fpeake, what was the reafon?
To praife thy friend, I hope, will not prove treafon !
Or was thy griefe fo great, thou didft conceale,
What neither tongue nor penne can well reveale ?
Or art[1] thou dead with him ? When a true friend
Is dead, what followes, but the other's end ?
Vberious *Horace*, had *Mæcenas* died,
Would not have writ nor fung, but onely cried :
Or if he needs muft fing, as well as cry,
H'ad done as Swans doe, onely fing and dy.
I might conclude, fince one's fo farre hence fled,
And th'other filent, that they both are dead.
Dead to their countrey both ; the one's not here,
The other (prefent) dares not fpeake for feare.
Which of thefe two is fureft flave to death ?
One breaths not, th'other dares not ufe his breath.
Pardon, if with the reft I filent be,
Great *Sutlin*, fince all Poets dyed in thee !
That he was valiant, none can better fhow,

Then

---

[1] [Original has *at.*]

Then can the valiant *Scot*, that was his Foe ;
That he was full fraught with all humane wit,
Will need no proof of mine : *Aglaura* doth it.
That hee was conftant ever unto the end,
Afke *Davenant* who was once, and ftill, his friend.
His hundred Horfes hoofes doe yet ftill ring
His liberall loyalty to his King.
Rip up this flefhy Cafket where there lay
Much gold, much filver, but much more of clay.
Nature did never make a piece fo rare,
Where all the Vertues met, each hath his fhare.
Some this, fome that ; fhould he give all thats beft
To one, that one would laugh at all the reft.
That he was noble, generous, open, free,
Is not deny'd, even by his enemy.
Which might have been approv'd too, as fome fay,
Even to the State, had he not runne away.
Ile not maintaine his Faults ; if any one
Lift, [he] may reade thefe Verfes on his Stone.
Whom many thoufand foes could not make fly,
Fled from his friends to France, and there did dye.

FINIS.

To Sir IOHN SVTLIN upon his

Aglaura : Firſt, a bloody Tragedy, then by

the ſaid Sir IOHN turn'd to a

COMEDIE.

When firſt I read thy Book, methought each word
Seem'd a ſhort Dagger, and each line a Sword.
Where Women, Men ; Good, Bad ; Rich, Poore—all dy :
That needs muſt prove a fatall Tragedy.
But when I finde, whom I ſo late ſaw ſlaine
In thy firſt Booke, in this revive againe,
I cannot but with others much admire
In humane ſhape a more then earthly Fire.
So when Prometheus did informe this Clay,
He ſtole his Fire from heaven.   What shall I ſay ?
Firſt for to Kill, and then to life reſtore,
This *Sutlin* did : the Gods can doe no more.